Teaching in the
Outdoors

Second Edition

by **Donald R. Hammerman**
Northern Illinois University
Dekalb, Illinois

and **William M. Hammerman**
California State University
San Francisco, California

BURGESS PUBLISHING COMPANY • MINNEAPOLIS, MINNESOTA

To the memory of L. B. Sharp,
who devoted his life to the
vision of education in the
out-of-doors

7   8   9   0

Foreword

This book, *Teaching in the Outdoors*, will aid greatly in learning and understanding those segments of the basic school curriculum that exist in the out-of-doors, for all subject matter areas at all grade levels.

There are many books available to aid teaching and learning in classrooms. These authors here present an effective guide to teaching in the out-of-doors.

In the early process of learning, method is more important than the specific knowledge. This does not imply that the end of learning is method only. The end is in the grasp and the understanding of specifics. Method does play a vital, if not a most important, part in how to arrive at the final truth.

The way one goes about learning, satisfying curiosity, and making discoveries in the out-of-doors requires many new teaching techniques. Thus, aids, suggestions, tips, ways to see and do, and interpretation of realities are the keys to effective learning and teaching outside the classroom. Methods which make it easier to learn, to remove fear of not knowing, to inspire one to keep going, are essential when extending education into the out-of-doors.

The authors have opened and laid an excellent trail bringing these outdoor education concepts into reality.

L. B. SHARP

Preface

During the past forty years, there has appeared on the American educational scene a curriculum development termed "outdoor education." This instructional movement has resulted in an increased number of schools utilizing the out-of-doors as laboratories for learning at the elementary, secondary, and higher education levels.

Continued expansion of outdoor education programs at all grade levels has presented a need for materials dealing with (1) the rationale underlying outdoor education; (2) the relationship of learning in the out-of-doors to the school curriculum; (3) effective techniques and procedures for outdoor teaching; (4) organizing, implementing, and evaluating resident outdoor school programs; and (5) implications for teacher education. This book lends itself for use by teachers-in-training, in-service teachers, school administrators, and college personnel. Organizational and private camp directors will also find *Teaching in the Outdoors* useful as a source for program ideas. This text may also suggest a means for extending the use of the summer camp facility into the school year.

The scope of the materials here is not intended to be an exhaustive coverage of the field or a collection of programs executed across the country. Rather it is a brief and concise point-of-view representing the philosophy of the authors derived from their personal experiences as professional outdoor educators.

The thoughts and information presented in this volume will, we trust, aid others in helping children and teachers to become better acquainted with "the strangeness of the familiar."

January, 1973   DRH
                                                                                    WMH

Contents

Chapter I
Why Education in
the Out-Of-Doors?

Every so often there hovers on the educational horizon a curriculum development of such import that only the pedagogical prophet or visionary is fully aware of its implication. The curriculum innovation which today carries the label "outdoor education" has not been without its prophets and visionaries. Over the years such educator-philosophers as Comenius, Rousseau, Pestalozzi, Herbart, Froebel, Spencer, Dewey, James, and Thorndike have pointed out the need for reinforcing abstract learning with concrete experience. The modern development of outdoor education is simply the current expression of this age-old educational axiom. As contemporary curriculum tends continually toward an emphasis on abstract knowledge, the need for holding onto concrete learning becomes increasingly important.

WHAT BASIC NEEDS ARE SERVED
BY OUTDOOR EDUCATION?

THE NEED FOR EFFECTIVE LEARNING

Outdoor education is an approach to more efficient and more effective learning. The purpose of outdoor education is to enrich, vitalize, and complement content areas of the school curriculum by means of firsthand observation and direct experience outside the classroom. Instruction which traditionally has been limited to the four walls of the classroom is, for the most part, highly verbal. Extending the classroom into the out-of-doors provides the setting for bringing deeper insight, greater understanding, and clearer meaning to those areas of knowledge which, ordinarily, are merely read and discussed—seldom experienced.

THE NEED FOR REALISM IN EDUCATION

Lord Chesterfield, in a letter to his son away at school, aptly advised him that "The knowledge of the world can only be acquired in the world, and not in a closet. Books alone will never teach you, but they will suggest many things to your observation." An effective teacher is one who can utilize all the resources at his disposal. These include the outdoor resources to be found in every community as well as the usual schoolroom resources.

There is no more highly stimulating setting than the "outdoor classroom." This classroom is equipped with expandable walls that extend as far as the learner's legs want to carry him, and a floor that varies from locale to locale—sometimes rocks, or water, sometimes forest floor. Its ceiling, too, is varied with ever changing cloud shapes, or at night with a myriad of star patterns

There is no substitute for firsthand observation.

waiting to be explored. No schoolroom ever had the books or maps or charts to rival the vividness of the real world.

Lessons of life are to be found at every hand in the outdoor classroom. The student does not need to content himself with mere words, symbols of reality, when he can see, touch, taste, smell, and hear living lessons that change with the seasons. Real understanding comes only through doing or experiencing. Children who have the opportunity to experience firsthand usually learn more rapidly. Furthermore, knowledge which is learned in this fashion is ordinarily retained far longer than that which is merely read about. Knowledge of the world in which we live cannot, as Chesterfield implied, be gained solely within the four walls of the classroom, no matter how expert the instructor or how comprehensive the curriculum.

A basic tenet of outdoor education stated by L. B. Sharp was "Teach outdoors that which can best be taught outdoors, and teach indoors that which can best be taught indoors." Educators all too frequently tend to transport subject matter out of its natural environment to the rather artificial confines of the classroom. Teaching out of context in this fashion invariably brings a certain amount of sterility to the classroom.

THE NEED FOR ENVIRONMENTAL LITERACY

Seldom has a movement become a universal cause célèbre more rapidly than the concern for environmental quality. Man pollutes his water, his air, his food, with the result that he pollutes himself. We are currently in an era when concern for man in his environment has become the number one priority.

The following definition was accepted at the "International Working Meeting on Environmental Education in the School Curriculum," held in conjunction with UNESCO's International Education Year in cooperation with UNESCO and the Foresta Institute for Ocean and Mountain Studies at Foresta Institute, Carson City, Nevada, June 20-July 10, 1970.

> Environmental education is the process of recognizing values and clarifying concepts in order to develop skills and attitudes necessary to understand and appreciate the interrelatedness among man, his culture and his biophysical surroundings. Environmental education also entails practice in decision-making and self-formulation of a code of behavior about issues concerning environmental quality.*

Man's survival may well depend upon his ability to control the pollutants with which he despoils the land. Rivers, lakes, and streams are dying. Air is not fit to breathe. Man himself multiplies to the point that his cities are no longer habitable. Despite cleanup campaigns, Earth Day, and environmental councils,

*This definition was developed by B. Ray Horn, at the time a member of the Department of Outdoor Teacher Education, Northern Illinois University.

degradation of the environment continues virtually unabated. The environment as it is presently constituted is fit neither for man or for living.

Emission controls on automobiles will help. Industrial smog controls will help. Zero population growth will help. Urban planning will help, and all are needed if man is to survive. The implications for education are clear. Senator Gaylord Nelson of Wisconsin advocated establishing environmental education programs that will make the environment and man's relationship to it a major subject at every level of public education. What could be more vital than to have students confronting and grappling with real problems rather than irrelevant, out-of-date, out-of-context exercises which comprise so many textbook assignments?

Many institutions of higher education have responded to the environmental crisis in the traditional manner by developing some nontraditional courses— Man, Nature, and Society; Urban Ecology; Biology and Human Affairs; History of Environmental Perception; The Social Impact of the Biological Scientist. Courses of study, seminars, conclaves, and conventions, in the main, attract only those who are strongly motivated to begin with. Legislation can prescribe rules and regulations to prevent gross misuse of the environment. Schools as a societal institution, however, are in the prime position to influence behavior, change attitudes, and develop guidelines and principles that will affect the masses. Learning activities in the outdoors designed to develop greater insight and understanding of ecological relationships and appreciation of man's responsibility for the quality of his environment should be part of the fabric from which new curricula are fashioned.

THE NEED FOR RE-CREATIVE EXPERIENCE

With a shortened work week pending, the American worker finds himself facing a greater number of "empty hours" than he has ever before encountered.

These hours, however, need not be "empty hours" to be filled with sedentary activity. Increased leisure may well provide the "vital hours" of one's existence—the hours to be lived for—spent in activity which enriches and fulfills life. The pressing need for wise use of leisure can surely be met, in part, through outdoor recreational skills such as boating, swimming, fishing, hunting, and camping. Likewise, since the findings of the President's Committee on Physical Fitness, there has been a resurgent interest in the physical well-being of America's youth. Healthful outdoor living can be a major contributing factor to improved physical fitness.

THE NEED FOR BASIC CONCEPTS

Further justification for outdoor education lies in the fact that concepts necessary for everyday living are more readily developed through firsthand learning. Concepts are tools for thinking. They enable man to think in terms of abstract ideas (truth, freedom, democracy) and class groupings (a robin is a bird, a bee is an insect). The ability to conceptualize also enables man to formulate a universally accepted idea of concrete things which he experiences directly in everyday living. Almost everyone, for example, has some idea of "tree," "bird," and "river," depending upon his tree, bird, and river experience.

During the middle childhood period (6-12 years) most individuals form several thousand concepts. Concepts learned in school at the verbal level are, all too often, mere words without meaning. Students very quickly learn that the right words in the right place at the right time will satisfy the teacher. Whether or not the pupil actually understands what he is saying frequently goes undetected, since his ability to use the right words appropriately is mistakenly accepted as evidence that learning has, in fact, taken place. Outdoor education provides the classroom teacher with a vehicle for providing real meaning to

abstract verbal learning, through direct experience. Pupils who go out into the schoolyard or to a nearby park to take a soil sample, test it, and analyze the results will have a far different concept of soil than pupils who are limited to reading about the soil of the Amazon River Valley in their geography books, and who still regard it as plain, ordinary dirt.

THE NEED FOR AWARENESS

There is a vital need, especially among the youth of today's "comic book, hot-rod, TV culture," to develop an awareness of the natural wonders of this amazing world. The modern youngster is missing a basic aspect of his own existence—acquaintance with the earth upon which he lives and depends for his livelihood and survival. Especially in this age of the supermarket, children ought to be aware of the sources from which they secure their food and, furthermore, should have an understanding of the natural forces upon which man depends for his needs, and their influence upon the economy.

The advent of television has served to bring worldwide marvels right into our living rooms; yet today's youth are largely ignorant of the mysteries of the earth, and its varied and marvelous inhabitants who live, reproduce, and die in our own back yards literally beneath our feet. A fascinating tableau of life in varied form from birth, to struggle for survival, to ultimate death is taking place in many backyards every day in the year. How many ever take the time to observe this never-ceasing drama? How many travel the exact same route to school or to work each day and are completely unfamiliar with, and for that matter unaware of natural phenomena (trees, flowers, birds nesting, insect life) along the way? One of the great contributions which outdoor education can make to this generation is to reestablish the fast-disappearing bond between man and the natural environment.

WHAT IS OUTDOOR EDUCATION?

To some people outdoor education is a somewhat vague and nebulous term. As a methodology or approach to more efficient and effective learning the term has been applied in various ways. It stands for a development in education that is difficult to pin down. To illustrate:

An agent from a midwestern Soil Conservation District office shows a group of Boy Scouts how wind and water combine to act as an erosive force in removing top soil from the corn fields of local farmers. To illustrate his point, he demonstrates with "splash sticks" just how much more water erosion is likely to take place when soil is left uncovered. Outdoor education enhances *conservation education*.

In Yosemite National Park, a ranger-naturalist explains to a group of summer vacationers how the valley floor was formed over many years by successive movements of glaciers. The group then hikes to various spots to observe the evidence—a "terminal moraine" and "glacial polish." Outdoor education enhances *science education*.

A second grade teacher in Maryland takes her class to a tobacco farm. Here, over a two-hour period of time, the children see how tobacco is cultivated, picked, and cured for marketing. Outdoor education enhances *agricultural education*.

In Michigan, a group of high school youths learn the skill involved in fly casting and archery during their physical education class periods. Outdoor education enhances *outdoor recreation*.

In the Sierra Nevada, a fifth grade class starts the school year with one week of camping. They fish, swim, hike, cook over an open fire, and sleep under the stars. The boys and girls make their own pack frames, construct their own shelters, and learn to live comfortably in a wilderness environment. Outdoor education enhances *camping education*.

Along a narrow path beside the shore of a lake in one of Indiana's many state parks, members of a seventh grade core class come upon some strange animal tracks leading from the water's edge to a hole in the ground. They make field sketches of the tracks and the entrance to the animal home, and several plaster casts of the tracks. The hiking group returns to the outdoor school's library to check their findings. They come to the tentative conclusion that the tracks were made by a raccoon. Still not positive of their identification, they rig up a self-tripping camera with flash at the entrance hole. The next morning, finding the trip sprung, they develop the film and confirm their "educated guess"—the animal is indeed a raccoon. Outdoor education enhances *nature study*.

A group of in-service teachers attend a summer workshop in which they "encounter" the quality of their environment through direct experiences in outdoor settings. One of the desired outcomes of the program is to assist each teacher to recognize and clarify the values, attitudes, and concepts necessary to understand and appreciate the interrelatedness among man, his culture, and his biophysical environment. In addition, these experiences are designed to provide him with the understandings and skills needed to contribute rationally to the decision-making process on issues involving the quality of the environment. Outdoor education enhances *environmental education.*

Miss Green was introducing her sixth graders to a social studies unit on "New World Explorers." During a discussion of navigational tools it was discovered that many members of the class did not know *how* or *why* a magnetic compass worked. For the science lesson that day, the teacher thought it wise to demonstrate with a suspended bar magnet just how a magnetized object will eventually swing to a north-south alignment. Before the session was over the youngsters had experimented enough to know about the magnetic field of force and the laws of attraction and repulsion. During the arithmetic period Miss Green introduced the idea of a circle with the degrees marked off which, placed beneath a freely swinging magnetized needle, becomes a compass. To reinforce the principle of a magnetic compass and to provide actual experience in using it as a directional tool, the class was taken out on the playground to determine the azimuths to various landmarks and to point out prescribed directions such as east, south-east, and 280°. It soon became apparent to the pupils that before a definite spot could be located, another element—distance—had to be known. After some firsthand acquaintance with surveyor's tapes each student learned how to determine the length of his own pace and was able to use this knowledge in estimating distances.

As a culmination of the exploration unit the boys and girls became modern-day explorers in the nearby city park. They organized into compass teams of three or four to collect directions and distances in order to make a map of the area. Once the field data were collected and recorded the class made a finished map of the area complete with title, scale, legend, north arrow, and declination. In order to check the accuracy of their field exercise they wrote a letter to the city park manager and invited him to visit the class and to bring along one of the city's official maps of the park for comparison purposes. Thus outdoor education *cuts across curriculum areas.*

It is obvious that outdoor education can be interpreted in a variety of ways. The conservationist, for example, looks upon the term as relating primarily to the wise use of natural resources. His chief concern is that of educating the public to the values of soil, water, forest, and wildlife resources and their wise management. The recreation leader, on the other hand, views outdoor education mainly as a means for realizing the joys of recreational pursuits in the out-of-doors. His approach would be one of educating youth to the ways of camping, fishing, and hunting. These outdoor recreational skills, naturally, have great carryover value for the adult years when people have real need for healthy leisure pursuits. The environmentalist sees outdoor education as a means of assisting each student in developing an attitude of personal responsibility toward his finite and fragile environment. One of the general goals of environmental education is to show that the conditions created by man through his social, economic, and technological systems have the proven capability of drastically altering the delicate biological community, and, as a result, the natural resources upon which life depends.

The classroom teacher considers outdoor education from still another viewpoint. Literally interpreted, the term means simply education, in a broad sense, which takes place in the out-of-doors. For our purposes outdoor education may be defined as "the utilization of the out-of-doors as a laboratory for learning." The diagram on page 10 illustrates the relationship between education in the out-of-doors and the school curriculum.

Those school-directed activities conducted outside the school building in an outdoor laboratory are, for our purposes, considered to be outdoor education experiences. Our interpretation of the definition might now be expanded to state that outdoor education is an approach toward achieving the goals and objectives of the curriculum which involves (1) an extension of the classroom to an outdoor laboratory; (2) a series of direct experiences in any or all phases of the curriculum involving natural materials and living situations which increase awareness of environment and life; (3) a program that involves pupils, teachers, and outdoor education resource people planning and working together to develop an optimum teaching-learning climate.

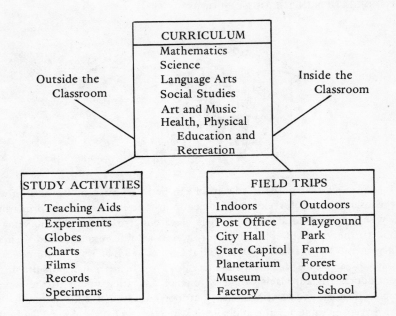

CURRICULUM

- Mathematics
- Science
- Language Arts
- Social Studies
- Art and Music
- Health, Physical Education and Recreation

Outside the Classroom

Inside the Classroom

STUDY ACTIVITIES

Teaching Aids
- Experiments
- Globes
- Charts
- Films
- Records
- Specimens

FIELD TRIPS

Indoors	Outdoors
Post Office	Playground
City Hall	Park
State Capitol	Farm
Planetarium	Forest
Museum	Outdoor
Factory	School

OUTDOOR EDUCATION

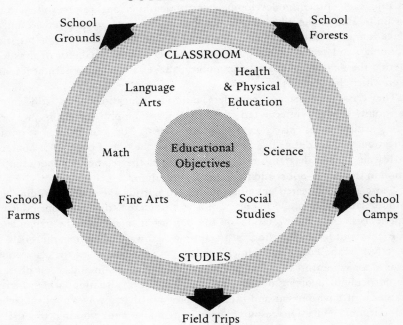

School Grounds

School Forests

CLASSROOM

Health & Physical Education

Language Arts

Math

Educational Objectives

Science

Fine Arts

Social Studies

School Farms

School Camps

STUDIES

Field Trips

Another diagram emphasizing the relationship between outdoor school laboratories, the school curriculum, and educational objectives appears at the bottom of page 10.

WHERE CAN OUTDOOR EDUCATION TAKE PLACE?

The out-of-doors abounds with areas appropriate for extending the classroom. Beginning just outside the classroom door and extending for miles in all directions, these unique learning laboratories have no equal. The schoolyard with trees, shrubbery, grass, and playground is available for activities lasting from a few minutes to one hour or more. Learning experiences of longer duration may be conducted at a nearby park, city zoo, or bird sanctuary. With a little exploration, the classroom teacher can locate many potential outdoor teaching sites inside the limits or within a few miles of almost any community.

Utilization of these various types of outdoor laboratories depends upon one's geographical location and the educational objectives desired. Field trips may be conducted with one major objective in mind, or with several goals cutting across several disciplines. The outdoor study activity may last from a few minutes to an hour or more, from a half day to one full day, or from two days to a week or longer. Extended field experiences take place at a resident outdoor school.

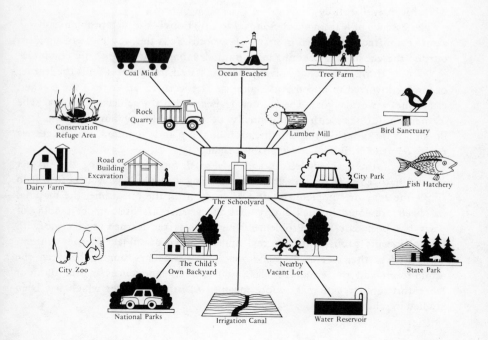

VALUES OF OUTDOOR EDUCATION

Out-of-classroom learning has a way of producing numerous gains, many of which defy measurement in terms of producing visible or tangible results. Among the list of intangible gains is the improved relationship that invariably develops between teacher and pupils. In the free atmosphere of the outdoor laboratory, unrestricted by the formalities of the schoolroom, pupils frequently view their teacher for the first time as an honest-to-goodness human being. Outdoor learning environments provide a setting which enables the teacher to observe his pupils in a variety of conditions in which he would not ordinarily see them. Under these circumstances a different sort of pupil-teacher relationship is bound to be established. In a day when the need for healthier human relationships between young and old, and among peoples of all races, creeds, and colors is paramount, the humanistic values derived from out-of-classroom learning experiences should not be overlooked.

Another prime value of out-of-classroom learning is that teachers and pupils have larger blocks of time (without the usual "in-school" interruptions such as bells ringing and classes changing) to come to grips with subject matter in some depth. Outdoor laboratories provide what may be considered almost the ideal academic setting—free of the usual interruptions, providing learners the framework for intensive study.

The essence of learning in these real-life situations is through problem solving, a process infrequently used in many classrooms. It is the way most of us learn outside the classroom. Learning in an outdoor laboratory is especially conducive to learning through problem solving. Briefly stated this process finds the learner becoming involved in purposeful planning. The learner, rather than the teacher, establishes a worthy goal. The learner devises a plan for achieving his goal. The learner, or learners, either individually or collectively try out the plan. If it doesn't work, a revision or modification of the plan is required, and successive trials are made until the desired goal is reached.

Much of the teaching effort today is so devoted to *covering* the subject matter that we fail to *uncover* the material being studied. Of what benefit is it to finish the text or complete the unit of study if, in the meantime, the material has been presented in such a way that the learner has little understanding of what has been covered? Problem-solving enables the learner to struggle with basic concepts fundamental to real understanding of subject matter content. This process then serves as a methodological pipeline running between the schoolroom and the extended classroom. Direct experiences in the outdoor laboratory enrich and make more meaningful subject matter which has been studied in school.

And here all these interesting animals lived together in the most copious and rural harmony; seldom if anywhere else in the world is such perfect and abject happiness to be found.

Everyone learns that teachers are people!

One element lacking in many curriculums today is the sheer joy of discovery. The classroom when extended into the outdoors provides the setting in which students may enjoy the pure thrill of discovery along with the plain, down-to-earth fun of learning. The learner is able to retrace and experience for himself the procedures and processes through which some of man's most significant discoveries of science, esthetics, and self have been made.

Another of the more tangible results that classroom teachers observe is an increased interest in what-is-in-the-book. After having captured an insect, or having found a rock specimen, or finally after much searching having located a single constellation in the night sky, a pupil is often motivated to turn eagerly and voluntarily to his textbooks in an effort to learn more about his discoveries. The quest for the *what*, the *how*, and the *why* of the world's mysteries can be an exciting adventure in learning, a never-ending search for the individual with an inquiring mind. As G. K. Chesterton once pointed out, "The world will never starve for want of wonders, but only for want of wonder."

SUMMARY

The concept of extending the classroom provides an instructional setting in which educators with imagination and vision may improve the calibre of instruction by making more meaningful, through direct experience and firsthand observation in the out-of-doors, that which is taught in the classroom.

The major theme of this chapter, "Why Education in the Out-of-Doors?" may be summarized along the following continuums.

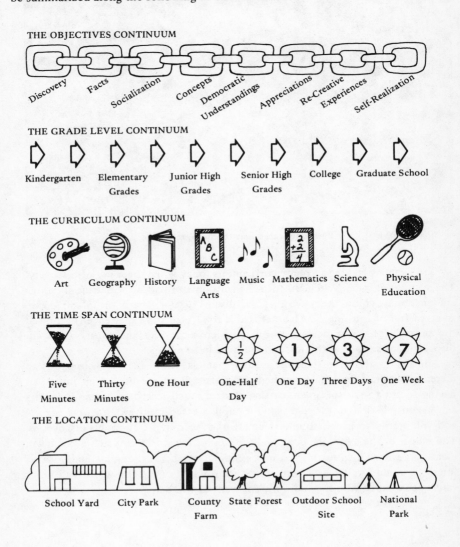

THE OBJECTIVES CONTINUUM

Discovery Facts Socialization Concepts Democratic Understandings Appreciations Re-Creative Experiences Self-Realization

THE GRADE LEVEL CONTINUUM

Kindergarten Elementary Grades Junior High Grades Senior High Grades College Graduate School

THE CURRICULUM CONTINUUM

Art Geography History Language Arts Music Mathematics Science Physical Education

THE TIME SPAN CONTINUUM

Five Minutes Thirty Minutes One Hour One-Half Day One Day Three Days One Week

THE LOCATION CONTINUUM

School Yard City Park County Farm State Forest Outdoor School Site National Park

SELECTED READINGS

AAHPER. *Outdoor Education for American Youth*. Washington: American Association for Health, Physical Education, and Recreation, 1957.

Bode, Boyd. "The Role of Camping in a Living Democracy." *Camping Magazine* 14:10-13, February, 1942.

*DeWitt, R. W. "Camping Education—A Philosophy." *National Elementary School Principal* 28:3-5, February, 1949.

Donaldson, George. *School Camping*. New York: Association Press, 1952.

*Donaldson, George W., and Louise E. Donaldson. "Outdoor Education—A Definition." *Journal of Health, Physical Education, Recreation* 29:17, 63, May, 1958.

Eliot, Charles W. "The Role of Camping in Social Life in a Changing World." *Camping Magazine* 14:20-21, February, 1942.

Freeberg, William, and Loren Taylor. *Philosophy of Outdoor Education*. Minneapolis: Burgess Publishing Company, 1961.

Harman, Dorothy C., et al. "What Is Outdoor Education?" *California Journal of Elementary Education* 26:71-78, November, 1957.

Hoffman, Betty. "School Camping Means Real-Life Learning." *National Education Association Journal* 38:360-61, May, 1949.

*Kilpatrick, William H. "The Role of Camping in Education Today." *Camping Magazine* 14:14-17, February, 1942.

Mackintosh, Helen K. "Why Camping and Outdoor Education Experiences in the School Program?" *Education Digest* 13:30-31, December, 1947.

*Masters, Hugh B. "Values of School Camping." *Journal of Health, Physical Education, Recreation* 22:14-15, January, 1951.

Nash, Jay B. "Why a School Camping Program." *Journal of Educational Sociology* 23:500-507, May, 1950.

Redl, Fritz. "The Role of Camping in Education." *Camping Magazine* 14:41-44, February, 1942.

Sharp, Lloyd B. "What Is Outdoor Education?" *School Executive* 71:19-22, August, 1952.

Sharp, Lloyd B. "Why Outdoor and Camping Education?" *Journal of Educational Sociology* 21:313-18, January, 1948.

Smith, Julian W. "Fitness Through Outdoor Education." *Journal of Health, Physical Education, Recreation* 28:10-11, September, 1957.

*____. "The Scope of Outdoor Education." *Bulletin of the National Association of Secondary School Principals* 44:156-58, May, 1960.

*Wheeler, Wallace, and D. Hammerman. "What Is the Educational Potential in the Outdoor Setting?" *Illinois Journal of Education* 55:2-4, December, 1965.

*These articles may be found in *Outdoor Education: A Book of Readings* by Hammerman and Hammerman (Minneapolis: Burgess Publishing Company, 1973).

Chapter II
Extending the School
Curriculum to the
Out-Of-Doors

Many content areas of the school curriculum can be enriched, comple-mented, or made more meaningful through firsthand observation and direct experience in the out-of-doors. A list compiled by classroom teachers of the kinds of experiences which they feel lend themselves well to teaching in the out-of-doors may be found on pp. 29-36.

An *exploratory approach* to learning is most appropriate in the outdoor classroom.* Children are innately curious and are inveterate collectors. The winding forest trail, a dried-up creek bed, a still woodland pond, a windblown field, or a dismal swamp beckon to the would-be explorer. The teacher need not feel inadequate because he lacks a science background; neither should he feel that he needs to be a naturalist to teach in the outdoor setting. Many of the same techniques that teachers use daily in their classrooms are adaptable and entirely suitable to the outdoor environment. A teacher who can skillfully turn children's questions back to them, causing them to look again, to examine more closely, to wonder "What happened here?" is capable of teaching in a variety of settings. A teacher does not have to know all the answers. Learning is a

*This teaching technique is discussed in detail in Chapter III.

cooperative venture. Pupils and teachers together seek explanations and under-standings of the many puzzles in the natural environment.

How are puzzles solved? How is knowledge gained? Most questions which a child asks can, in turn, be answered by the questioner after close, careful, firsthand investigation. How can observational skills be taught? Consider the following example. A group has stopped along the trail to rest. The teacher asks each hiker to mark off one square foot. Each person then has five minutes or so to explore intensively his one foot square territory. The object is to find as many different natural phenomena as possible. It isn't necessary for the individual to identify his "finds" at this time; the main purpose is to develop "seeing eyes." After the initial investigation, each child tallies the number of "discoveries" he has made. Interesting specimens may be described to the entire group. Additional interest can be stimulated by the instructor through leading ques-tions. For example: "How many found some moss in their one foot square territory?" "Let's see how many different types of moss we have found." "Would you like to preserve some of these mosses so that we can take them back to the classroom to find out more about them?" "We can keep mosses and other small plants alive for a year or even longer." "Have you ever made a glass-jar terrarium?" Thus a new and exciting learning activity is under way.

The "ABC Scavenger Hunt" is another way to enlarge upon the ability to see and find that which has always been underfoot. Divide the class into small groups of not more than four or five. Let each group select a leader, who then lists the alphabet from top to bottom on a sheet of paper. The idea then is to find one nature item for as many of the letters in the alphabet as possible. Students often find items such as:

A—acorn, ant, aspen leaf
B—bug, bark, beetle
C—clay, cricket, cherry

Among elementary and even secondary school pupils this activity presents an opportunity for vocabulary development. An acorn, for example, might also count for N—nut, S—seed, F—fruit.

It is highly desirable to bring as many senses as possible into play in developing an initial awareness to the out-of-doors. Stopping—absolutely still—to listen for a whole minute is a new experience for many children. The challenge is to discover how many different "sounds" can be "tuned in" during one listening minute. It is not vital that each sound be named. Some children may hear four or five distinctly different bird songs and not be able to name even one. The important point is that they have heard the songs, and have distinguished them as being different. The next step in this exploratory activity is to follow one's ears until the mystery singer can be sighted and identified.

Another sense perception which children can heighten on an exploratory hike is feeling. They can feel their way along the trail for awhile—from tree to tree—for example. Each person closes his eyes as he approaches a new tree, and pauses to explore the trunk with his hands. "Is this bark rougher, or smoother than the last?" "If you had to choose one word to describe its 'feel' or texture, what would that word be? Ridged, pebbly, scratchy, flaky, silky?" Again an opportunity is presented to expand vocabulary, while at the same time allowances are made for individual interpretation. The same exploratory approach can be applied to leaves and rocks in terms of, "What does it feel like to you?" "How would you describe what you are examining so that another person could recognize it from your description?"

Another sense frequently overlooked is that of taste. Caution should be exercised, however, to ensure that children are not encouraged to taste something which might prove harmful. If the leader is unsure, it is safer to pursue a policy of no tasting.

Still another sense which can be utilized in developing an initial awareness to the out-of-doors is the sense of smell. Have you ever tried smelling your way along the trail? Crush a leaf, or lift a handful of moist earth from beneath the leaf mold, or break open a fruit and sniff. The more senses one can involve as he explores his way into the "real world" outdoors, the more vivid will be his perceptions.

What has actually happened in each of these instances? A teacher has been teaching, and pupils have been learning; teaching and learning have taken place in an outdoor classroom. The children were "close to what they were learning about" and were "seeing what they had read about." The teacher was not passing on knowledge by mere verbal description, but was facilitating the acquisition of knowledge by acquainting the children with the subject matter through a face-to-face confrontation.

Nearly all areas of the curriculum may be complemented with appropriate learning experiences in the outdoor laboratory. This outdoor classroom may be a

schoolyard, a nearby park, a forest preserve, or an outdoor school site. The way in which the outdoor experience is related to the curriculum may be highly organized and structured or unstructured and informal, depending upon the individual teacher, the time available, the site, and the purposes to be achieved. In the above examples of learning in the out-of-doors, the connections between these experiences and science, language arts, arithmetic, and problem-solving may readily be seen. Music, art, reading, and writing could be integrated with these firsthand learning experiences through appropriate follow-up activities back in the schoolroom.

Even in a highly structured program it often happens that, in the interest of more effective learning, it is wise to forget original plans and take advantage of the "teachable moment." For example, while on a trip to explore the geological formations down by the lake, eight girls and boys with their instructor spotted some tadpole eggs near the water's edge. The eggs hadn't hatched yet; they appeared to be jellylike marbles with a baby "polliwog" inside each one. Very carefully, one of the children transferred a few of the eggs and some lake water to a container, so that they could be taken back to the home base for further observation and for the rest of the class to see. Shortly thereafter the eggs began to hatch. The wiggly black babies ruptured their bubblelike prisons and darted

This is a far cry from the sights and smells of crowded city streets.

free into the water. After a few minutes, every egg had produced one tadpole, and every pupil had observed one of the natural science world's most fascinating phenomena—birth. One girl was motivated to create a poem about the event. A boy made plans for constructing a permanent container so that newly hatched "polliwogs" could be properly cared for in the classroom for continued study and observation before being returned to their natural habitat.

Another group of pupils utilized the out-of-doors as a source for problems in mathematics. They were quite familiar with the "word problems" in their arithmetic textbook back in the classroom, but here they were solving "live" problems that they could actually visualize in space and distance rather than words alone. Earlier in the afternoon they had solved the exercises planned by the teacher, "How large is an acre?" and "How many board feet of lumber does that tree contain?" After having paced off their one-acre plots and having learned the use of the Biltmore stick and Merritt rule in figuring board feet of lumber, the pupils were returning to their meeting place via the River Trail when one of the girls said, "I wonder how wide this river is?" While they were contemplating this problem, another pupil asked, "Which way is the river flowing?" and another questioned, "How fast is the water moving?" Within a few minutes, the pupils were confronted with an entirely new series of arithmetic-related problems. By inductive reasoning, the teacher assisted the children in developing techniques that led to the solution of their questions concerning the river.

The variety and number of valuable learning activities which can be carried on in the extended classroom out-of-doors is virtually limitless. These activities may be structured according to subject matter areas of the school curriculum, or they may be approached topically. Still another variation is to organize the outdoor learning activities on a seasonal or a unit basis.

THINGS TO SEE AND DO
WHEN THE LEAVES TURN COLOR

STUDY THEMES:

- What causes the autumn season?
- Why do birds and some insects travel such great distances at this time of year?
- How is the weather changing?
- How are plants changing? Why are they changing?
- How are the animals preparing for the winter?

THINGS TO DO:

- Watch for flocks of birds. Identify them if possible. Record the date observed and approximate number of birds sighted.
- Keep a daily weather record noting maximum and minimum temperatures.

- Record time of sunrise and sunset. Log the hours of daylight.
- Examine seeds under a hand lens. Note seed structure and relationship to the mode of transportation. Observe and record seed travels.
- Dig a small trench to note depth of the frost line.
- Collect weeds for bouquets.
- Collect seeds and leaves.
- Watch caterpillars make cocoons. Put a cocoon in a box outdoors, and watch the moth emerge in the spring.

THINGS TO SEE AND DO WHEN THE SNOW FALLS

STUDY THEMES:

- Where and how do insects and animals spend the winter?
- What constellations are visible in the night sky?
- What causes the winter season?
- How do plants survive the winter?

THINGS TO DO:

- Investigate deserted bird nests to see how they are constructed.
- Follow animal tracks in the snow. Measure the tracks, and sketch them.
- Sharpen senses on nature trails every season by specializing in listening on one trip, looking on another, touching, tasting, and smelling.
- Identify animal tracks and homes.
- Set up bird feeding stations. Observe and record the birds that feed on them.
- Continue recording weather data.
- Record azimuth for the position of sunset for a month. Note the direction of movement.
- Examine snowflakes and frost crystals under magnification.
- Measure snow depth and convert to inches of rainfall.

THINGS TO SEE AND DO WHEN THE SAP FLOWS

STUDY THEMES:

- How is the weather changing?
- What changes are taking place in plants?
- What is soil? How does man use the soil?
- How do plants and animals help one another?
- How does man use plants and animals?

THINGS TO DO:

- Choose a tree and study all life around it as spring changes.
- Watch for the return of birds, first leaves, first flowers, first insects. Observe and record dates.
- Watch the changing cloud forms in the sky. Sketch the different cloud types.
- Watch a pair of birds building a nest. Observe them and record their activities.
- Sketch or photograph a treebud as it first unfolds in the spring.
- Record the changing position of the sun at sunset each day for several weeks.

Any realistic approach to making best use of the out-of-doors as a teaching medium must give serious consideration to the unique features of the local area in which the learning activities are to be carried out. Several examples of this type of planning appear below.

THINGS TO SEE AND DO WITH HILLS AND VALLEYS

The hills and valleys of this area are the result of the melting of the last continental glacier which retreated from the northern states about 20,000 years ago. This great, continental glacier stood in Wisconsin some 50 miles to the north. As the glacier melted it liberated great quantities of stone and earth that it had carried with it from as far north as the interior of Canada. The melting of the ice mass also liberated vast quantities of water. This water, discharging down the river valley, carried with it sand and gravel, and clay. The murky waters carried the clay onward to the Gulf of Mexico, but much of the sand and gravel was dropped along the course of the great stream across this area.

THINGS TO DO:

- On your hike look for rocks that have scratches on them made by a glacier. These are called glacial striations.
- Follow a gully to its source. Look for evidence of erosion.
- Estimate the depths of the valleys in this area.
- Make a map showing the southern limits of the glacier.

CAN YOU FIND OUT?

- What is a continental glacier?
- Where and how do glaciers originate?
- Where does a glacier pick up rocks, sand, and gravel?
- What causes glaciers to melt?

THINGS TO SEE AND DO WITH GULLY EROSION

Directly north and east of the outdoor education area there is a large gully.

THINGS TO DO:

- Examine a cross section of soil in the gully. See if you can recognize the different layers.
- Gather various samples of topsoil and subsoil.
- As you hike along the gully look for an example of a pothole formed by running water.
- Go to the mouth of the gully and examine the miniature delta that has formed there. Identify the various kinds of sedimentary material which have been washed down the gully.

CAN YOU FIND OUT?

- What is topsoil? What does it consist of?
- What is subsoil? What are its main ingredients?
- What causes soil to wash away?
- How can a gully be stopped from getting larger?

THINGS TO SEE AND DO WITH WILDLIFE

A great variety of animals including chipmunk, squirrel, oppossum, moles, raccoon, fox, rabbit, and deer live in the area.

THINGS TO DO:

- Follow some animal tracks. See if you can reconstruct the story, and tell where the animal was going.
- Collect animal tracks by making plaster casts or sketching them.
- Look for animal homes: rock dens, hollow trees, and ground burrows.
- Look for evidence of what animals feed on: bark stripped from young trees, empty nut husks, and ground diggings.

CAN YOU FIND OUT?

- What kind of tracks do deer, rabbit, raccoon make?
- What kinds of homes do these animals live in?
- What do they eat?
- How do they spend the winter?

THINGS TO SEE AND DO WITH ASTRONOMY

Winter months are the best for observing the stars.

THINGS TO DO:

- Draw pictures and star maps of constellations so that you will be able to recognize them in the sky.
- Read stories about the constellations.
- Photograph star trails by taking a two-hour time exposure of the Northern Hemisphere.

CAN YOU FIND OUT?

- What constellations will be appearing in the sky during the time you are at the Outdoor School? Remember that the date and hour of the observation is important, since constellations appear to move across the sky as the earth rotates from west to east.
- Will the moon be visible during your stay at the Outdoor School? If so, what phase will it be in?
- Will any planets be visible at this time?

THINGS TO SEE AND DO
WITH ROCKS, MINERALS, AND FOSSILS

The gully is a treasure house of rocks and fossils.

THINGS TO DO:

- Hunt for rocks, minerals, and fossils.

- Test various specimens to find differences in hardness, color, luster, streak, and fracture.

CAN YOU FIND OUT?

- What are the three main classes of rocks?
- How do rocks change from one kind to another?
- What is a mineral?
- How are fossils formed?

THINGS TO SEE AND DO WITH BIRD LIFE

Depending upon the season of the year, migratory birds and resident species can be found in the outdoor classroom.

THINGS TO DO:

- Investigate many bird books to find out what particular birds you should see at this time of year.
- Collect pictures and make sketches of birds that you expect to see. This will help you to recognize them.

Birds welcome.

- Find an old, *unoccupied* bird nest. Examine it closely and extract a sample of each kind of material which the bird has used in constructing it.

CAN YOU FIND OUT?

- What birds eat so that you may maintain a feeding station outside your classroom?
- Why certain birds migrate during the spring and the fall of the year?

THINGS TO SEE AND DO FOR ENVIRONMENTAL QUALITY

Citizens, young and old alike, can work effectively for a better environment only to the extent that they understand those factors which contribute to the degradation of the environment.

THINGS TO DO:

- Visit your local water purification plant.
- Take a field trip to the watershed area for your community.
- Visit a recycling center.
- Take an aerial field trip over your community: observe the traffic patterns, housing developments, and open land space.
- Take pictures of some of the most offensive eyesores in your community and submit them to the local newspaper.
- Write articles for the local paper offering suggestions for cleaning up the environment.

CAN YOU FIND OUT?

- How is the sewage treated in your community?
- To what extent are lakes, rivers, ponds, and streams in your county polluted?
- How do hunting and fishing laws help to maintain the quality of environment?
- What are the kinds of environmental problems that affect people in the large cities?
- What is the percentage of land in your community devoted to the needs of the automobile (freeways, streets, parking areas, etc.)?
- What is the amount of noise in a nearby residential area, business area, and an industrial area?

THINGS TO SEE AND DO WITH AIR

THINGS TO DO:

- Visit an air pollution control district's measuring station.

- Develop a "dirty-air" index using vaseline and shining paper.
- Design a visual aid that illustrates the oxygen/carbon dioxide cycle.

CAN YOU FIND OUT?

- What causes smog?
- How does air pollution affect human beings?
- What are the air quality control standards of your area?
- What does it cost your community to meet clean air standards?

THINGS TO SEE AND DO WITH WATER

THINGS TO DO:

- Visit a watershed area for the water supply of your community.
- Visit a nearby stream and measure its rate of speed.
- Visit a body of water that might be polluted.
- Develop a visual aid that illustrates the water cycle.

CAN YOU FIND OUT?

- What plant and animal life exists near the stream?
- What animals live in the stream?
- What is the temperature of the water?
- What is the pH number of the water?
- What is the estimated dissolved oxygen content of the water?
- Is this water safe to drink?
- Where does your community dispose of its liquid wastes?

THINGS TO SEE AND DO WITH SOIL

THINGS TO DO:

- Visit a road cut or excavation in order to observe the soil profile.
- Construct a soil micromonolith of a soil profile.
- Observe a stream that is cutting away at its bank.
- Develop projects that will prevent soil erosion by wind and rain.

CAN YOU FIND OUT?

- Can you see the various layers of soil in the profile?
- What things live in the top layer of soil?
- How does the soil temperature vary from layer to layer?
- Determine the pH of each layer.
- Determine the color, texture, and structure of each major layer.
- Determine the water-holding capacities of various soils.
- How much soil is lost in your area due to erosion?

OUTDOOR LEARNING ACTIVITIES
RELATED TO THE SCHOOL CURRICULUM

The number of experiences that can be carried out in the outdoor classroom in connection with the school curriculum is limited only by the imagination of the teacher. Following are a few examples of outdoor education activities that have proved successful and significant to children in the field.

ARITHMETIC

General Objectives

A. To use standard measuring instruments (compass, ruler, tape, gallon, etc.)
B. To understand relationship of arithmetic to everyday living.
C. To develop capacity to estimate (distance, time, quantity, space, etc.).
D. To apply arithmetic skills to firsthand experiences in the outdoors.

Things to Do

- Cutting and piling a cord of wood.

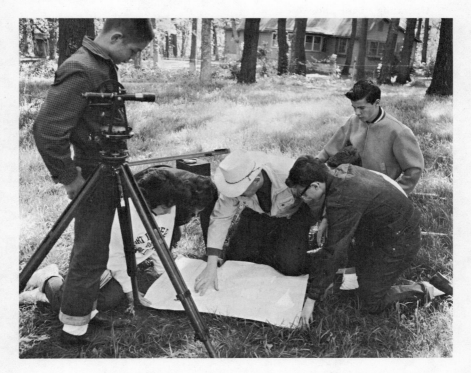

Pupils learn that mathematics has its practical side, too.

- Measuring: a board foot, age of tree through ring count.
  - circumference and diameter of trees.
  - surface area for map making, scale drawings, or models.
  - dimensions of camp buildings.
  - percent of slope.
  - distances between buildings, trees.
  - distance in hiking, by pacing.
- Estimating: height of tree, hill.
  - time of day.
  - distance hiked.
  - distance away of lightning.
  - width of river.
- Averaging: temperature readings.
  - barometric readings.
- Compass hiking.
- Planning amounts and costs of food for cookouts.
- Figuring finances for the experience.
- Construction of stiles, shelters, check dams, bridges, feeding stations.
- Operating a bank and store.
- Computing the amount of open space in your community.

LANGUAGE ARTS

General Objectives

A. To write legibly and spell correctly.
B. To express oneself well in both written and spoken word.
C. To read and interpret correctly.

Things to Do

- Writing letters home.
- Planning the weekly program.
- Keeping field notes.
- Using the library for research reading.
- Enjoying a good book in free time.
- Labeling and identifying specimens.
- Dramatizations.
- Writing of poems, diaries, logs, newspapers, stories, songs, menus.
- Story telling.

SOCIAL STUDIES

General Objectives

A. To create an interest in and understanding of local history.

B. To develop an understanding of democratic procedures and of group processes.
C. To create an understanding of the relationship between man and his environment.
D. To develop an understanding of some of the socio-emotional needs of man.
E. To develop an understanding of how a local government functions.

Things To Do

- Looking for Indian relics.
- Construction of pioneer buildings, household articles.
- Making a community study of some small community nearby.
- Visiting local spots of historical interest.
- Making craft items out of natural materials.
- Map and model making.
- Putting on a pageant about a local historical event.
- Participating in an Indian ceremonial.
- Making of traps, snares, slings, boomerangs, etc.
- Visiting an abandoned farm.
- Participating in camp government.
- Cooperation in camp activities.
- Dramatizing conversations among Indians, pioneers.
- Photographing examples of man's misuse of his environment.
- Developing a land-use map of your community.

NATURAL SCIENCES

Plant and Animal Life

General Objectives

A. To be able to recognize some of the common plants and animals in the local area.
B. To understand some of the interrelationships of plant and animal life in different environments of the local area.
C. To know various methods of seed dissemination.
D. To know the uses of different plants and animals.
E. To understand the need for conservation of plant and animal life.

Things to Do

- Making clue charts for identification of trees, flowers, birds.
- Collecting and pressing leaves and other plentiful plant specimens.
- Collecting and mounting seeds, insects.
- Leaf study by means of blue prints, potato prints, spatter prints, crayon, clay.
- Studying animal tracks, making clay molds.

- Sketching.
- Using microscope and hand lens for closer scrutiny of parts.
- Nature scavenger or treasure hunts.
- Building shelters and feeding stations.
- Observing animals and keeping field notes on habits.
- Collecting old bird nests and studying their construction.
- Finding animal homes.
- Taking nature hikes.
- Building a terrarium or aquarium.
- Learning to recognize bird and animal sounds.
- Using plant, tree, and animal products to make: cooking utensils, cordage, whistles, fishing plugs, tea, jewelry.
- Tapping maple trees.
- Listening to night sounds.
- Diagramming food chains for various animals.
- Calculating food pyramids for different species.
- Conducting study plot explorations over a period of time.
- Replanting seedlings in a burned-out area.

There is more to a weather report than merely looking at the daily paper.

EARTH SCIENCE

General Objectives

A. To understand some general characteristics of rock strata in the local area as they relate to plants, animals, and water.
B. To understand the history of rocks and their contribution to soil formation.
C. To understand the relationship of surface terrain to underlying rock strata.
D. To understand the causes, effects, and ways to control erosion.
E. To be able to recognize some major constellations and their relationship to earth motions.
F. To understand the nature and movements of heavenly bodies as a pattern of related behavior.
G. To understand forces in weather events.

Things to Do

- Collecting rocks, soils, and fossils.

Will it, or won't it? Fizz, that is.

- Visiting a quarry or gravel pit.
- Walking up gullies, studying rocks, soil, effects of erosion.
- Breaking up a rock and studying its properties under microscope.
- Keeping field notes of observations on a locale before and after rain.
- Taking a rain hike.
- Conducting soil experiments: test for acidity or alkalinity.
- Studying a slope at different elevations: using a hand level to measure elevations.
- Visiting a conservation farm to observe good conservation practices.
- Night study of major constellations.
- Looking at moon through binoculars or telescope.
- Constructing a soil micromonolith.
- Recording phases of moon.
- Looking for meteorites.
- Estimating time by shadow of sun or by star position.
- Making star trails with camera.
- Observing and sketching clouds.
- Building weather instruments.
- Making weather observations and predictions.
- Conducting air and water experiments.
- Visiting game and forest preserves.
- Visiting a fish hatchery.

HEALTH, PHYSICAL EDUCATION, AND RECREATION

General Objectives

A. To develop wholesome mental attitudes and habits.
B. To practice good health habits.
C. To plan and practice wholesome use of leisure time.
D. To keep physically fit.
E. To develop an awareness of safe practices in the outdoors.
F. To integrate health and physical education with other subject matter areas.

Things to Do

- Planning healthy meals.
- Dressing properly and adequately for different occasions.
- Discussing and solving group living problems.
- Practicing outdoor safety:
  how to go up and down a hill;
  how to carry and use lumbering tools, jack knife;
  being sure that water is safe to drink;
  care of fire on cookouts.
- Dancing (pioneer, square, round, Indian, folk, play-party games).

- Carrying out service projects such as:
  building a retaining wall;
  developing outpost sites;
  cutting firewood;
  setting tables;
  making beds;
  keeping buildings clean;
  clearing underbrush;
  establishing fire stations.
- Fishing.
- Playing games such as:
  Skittles;
  Stalking a deer;
  Duck on the rocks;
  Up Jenkins;
  Indian corn game;
  Japanese checkers;
  Capture the flag;
  Huckle buckle bean stalk.
- Enjoying winter sports such as:
  ice fishing;
  skating;
  skiing;
  making and using snowshoes.

ARTS, CRAFTS, AND MUSIC

General Objectives

A. To give a child an opportunity to explore a variety of media (with emphasis on natural materials).
B. To encourage the child to express his imaginative ideas as well as his realistic ones.
C. To develop interests, information, and skills in art and music which will lead to profitable use of leisure time.
D. To consider art and music as a part of everyday living.
E. To develop handiness with common tools.
F. To show relationship of art and music to cultures of different people.
G. To get everyone in the group to sing for the fun of it.
H. To develop a feeling for and understanding of rhythm.

Things to Do

- Making game equipment.
- Making simple camp furniture.

- Drawing a map of camp area, compass maps of hikes.
- Making picture frames.
- Sketching, drawing, coloring, painting gullies, streams, landscapes, camp scenes, etc.
- Observing, counting color tones in distance.
- Clay work (modeling, making molds).
- Wood carving, chipping, whittling.
- Making bouquets, corsages.
- Collecting weeds, seeds, grasses, feathers, etc. (to make arrangements).
- Making drums, rattles, tom-toms, headdresses for Indian ceremonial.
- Weaving grasses, barks, reeds, etc.
- Taking photographs.
- Tree fungus carving.
- Singing songs and rounds.
- Marching, dancing, skipping, clapping, leaping to music recordings, drum beatings, songs, etc.
- Composing songs.
- Listening to night sounds and comparing with recordings of such.
- Imitating bird calls.
- Matching tones.
- Playing singing games.
- Looking for familiar objects in cloud formations.
- Painting, photographing, or drawing the same scene in different seasons.
- Making and playing on primitive instruments.
- Listening to music recordings.

SUMMARY

The creative teacher opens an entirely new world of realistic teaching-learning situations when he steps beyond the classroom door into the out-of-doors. The myriad of educational opportunities guarantees relevant topics and exciting activities for students at all grade levels. Although a variety of organizational plans may be utilized (topical, seasons of the year, subject matter areas, or problem areas) the significant factor is that the teacher extends the learning experiences of the curriculum to the out-of-doors.

SELECTED READINGS

AAHPER. *Outdoor Education for American Youth.* Washington: American Association for Health, Physical Education, and Recreation, 1957.
Association for Classroom Teachers. *Man and His Environment.* Washington, D.C.: National Education Association, 1970.

Bale, Robert O. *Conservation for Camp and Classroom*. Minneapolis: Burgess Publishing Company, 1962.

Carroll, John S. "Camping Education Can Vitalize the Entire School Program." *Nation's Schools* 45:28-31, June, 1950.

Clark, L. S. "Woodland Areas as Outdoor Laboratories." *School Science and Mathematics* 61:713-14, December, 1961.

Danner, Katherine S., and Marsha A. Reid. *A Manual for Study Plot Exploration*. P.O. Box 1336, Bloomington, Ind. 47401, 1971.

Dodge, John E. "Conservation on Location." *National Education Association Journal* 46:262-4, April, 1957.

*Donaldson, George W., and Hope A. Lambert. "School Camp—Outdoor Laboratory for Enriched Learning Experiences." *Camping Magazine* 28:17-21, May, 1956.

Freeberg, William, and Loren Taylor. *Programs in Outdoor Education*. Minneapolis: Burgess Publishing Company, 1962.

Greenspan, Arthur. "Camping in the School Curriculum." *Instructor* 66:74, June, 1957.

Hug, John, and Phyllis Wilson. *Curriculum Enrichment—Outdoors*. New York: Harper & Row Publishers, 1966.

McClusky, Howard Y. "The Out of Doors as Part of the Total Educational Program." *School Executive* 64:63-65, February, 1945.

Milliken, Margaret, et al. *Field Study Manual for Outdoor Learning*. Minneapolis: Burgess Publishing Company, 1968.

Pike, K. V. "Natural Science Experience Significant to Elementary Programs of Outdoor Education." *Science Education* 46:141-5, March, 1962.

Smith, Julian W. *Outdoor Education*. Washington, D.C.: American Association for Health, Physical Education, and Recreation, 1956.

Swan, Malcolm D., ed. *Tips and Tricks in Outdoor Education*. Danville, Ill.: Interstate Printers and Publishers, 1970.

Van Til, William A. "Schools and Camping." *Toward a New Curriculum*. Washington, D.C.: American Association for Supervision and Curriculum Development, 1944.

Vessel, Matthew F., and Arnold G. Applegarth. *Experiments With Living Things*. Palo Alto, Calif.: Fearon Publishers.

Chapter III
Techniques of Teaching
in the Out-Of-Doors

An approach to teaching which is virtually synonymous with outdoor education is that which we have termed the "exploratory" or "discovery" approach to learning. The essence of this teaching procedure is the systematic use of questioning to provoke thoughtful observation and reaction on the part of the learner. Socrates employed this technique most effectively.

The learner is led to explore unknown objects and processes in the natural environment. Through skillful questioning he is guided to look for himself and to see, to think about what he has observed, to integrate and synthesize the significant elements of his observations until he is able to formulate a reasonable conclusion as to "What happened here?" He acquires knowledge through the use of the resources and materials of reality rather than through mere verbal dissemination of factual content. Telling, alone, is not teaching. Teaching calls for the involvement of the learning organism in experiencing. In this way the student is motivated to utilize all of his senses (multisensory learning) in seeking answers to the countless mysteries which confront his every step along the outdoor path of learning. He substitutes his own direct experience in the form of sights, sounds, odors, tastes, and feelings for symbols in a text, and thus enhances and makes more meaningful the great mass of verbal knowledge to which he has already been exposed.

Writer-naturalist Edwin Way Teale has said, "The strangeness of the familiar is too familiar to be observed." It is to help the learner become aware of "the strangeness of the familiar" and to incorporate these discoveries into his own system of appreciations and understandings that an exploratory approach to learning can be most effectively employed by the teacher out-of-doors.

Let us focus more precisely upon the role of the teacher when applied to specific outdoor teaching situations.

INQUIRY IN AN OUTDOOR LABORATORY*

As an instructional approach for "finding out," inquiry embodies elements of other approaches to learning which have carried various labels, such as problem solving, discovery method, exploratory approach, Socratic method, leading question technique, nondirective approach, and so on. Whatever label it bears, this approach to the teaching-learning process has one basic aim, namely, to *involve* the learner *in* and *with experience* to the extent that he is able to formulate his own questions, seek his own answers—in other words, to enable the learner to find out for himself.

Time and again we are told that *telling is not teaching* and yet we persist with verbal inundation which drowns the learner in a sea of words. A simple example will serve to contrast these two approaches.

Picture this scene: The setting is a sixth grade classroom. The teacher, Mr. Glib-Gab, is holding forth in his usual style. "Class, today I'm going to tell you about a fossil that I found on my vacation last summer. This is called a cephalopod. Its origin was an ancient Ordovician sea some 360 to 420 million years ago.

"The word fossil means to dig up. It is derived from the Latin word *fodere* which translates 'to dig up.' Originally, the word fossil referred to most anything of mineral composition or of unusual form that was dug from the ground. Today, however, the word fossil means any direct evidence of past life. Other examples, besides this bit of marine life, would include ancient clam shells, dinosaur bones, a plant impression, or the footprints of an extinct animal.

"Most of the time we find fossils in sedimentary rock such as mudstone, shale, limestone, sandstone, dolomite, and conglomerate. They may also be found in some igneous and metamorphic rocks. There is one rock that is composed almost completely of fossils. It is called *coquina*."

This scene, or one much like it, is an all too common occurrence in the modern classroom. This teacher's monologue more than likely could have continued for quite some time. There was little or no opportunity for pupils to interact with one another as inquirers or with the object of study itself.

By way of contrast, let us shift the scene to an outdoor learning situation. The setting is a gully. The gully twists and turns so that you can't quite see around the next bend. This very characteristic, it seems, makes you want to see

*Adapted from *Instructor*, ©1970, Instructor Publications, Inc.

what is around the next bend. The gully floor is covered with rocks that have been carried along intermittently by the rushing torrent which charges headlong to the river with each rain. The gully is a hunting ground filled with countless treasure. Today it is also filled with eager children—eager because they are exploring on their own. They have managed to get out from between the two covers of the textbook.

For the purpose of illustration we will focus on the dialogue between the teacher, Mr. Catalyst, and one of his pupils.

Pupil: Holy cats, Mr. C., look what I've found! What is it?

Mr. C: Well, I don't know for sure. Let's take a closer look at it. (Mr. C. knows, he just isn't saying.) Here, look at it under this magnifying glass. What do you see?

Pupil: Well, I see a shell. It looks like a clam shell.

Mr. C: Look again. Is it actually a shell?

Pupil: Gosh no! There's no shell material. It's just an imprint on this rock. I wonder how it got there.

Mr. C: What else do you see?

Pupil: I see a lot of small grains.

Mr. C: What do they look like to you?

Pupil: It looks like cement, or sand maybe.

Mr. C: Here, let's scrape a little off with my knife. Now feel this. What does it feel like?

Pupil: It feels like sand. Yes, it's sand all right. This must be sandstone. I still wonder, though, how the shell imprint got in the stone. It must have taken tremendous pressure.

Mr. C: Yes, you're right. Let's pursue this a little bit further to see if I can help you figure out the rest of the puzzle. Where do you ordinarily find shells?

Pupil: Oh, along the beach. We go to Wildwood, New Jersey, each summer, and I've found loads of shells. In fact, some of them even look like this one.

Mr. C: All right, now give this careful thought. See if you can use all the evidence we have thus far to solve this mystery. There once was a shell and now it is gone, but we have a clue in this fossil. What happened here?

Pupil (after considerable head scratching and brow wrinkling):
Well, here's what I think happened. Shells are found by the shore, and the waves wash them back and forth. Sometimes they're washed up on the shore, and some shells are washed back out to sea. I've watched the sand wash over the shells at the beach. I've seen some shells sort of burrow down into the sand, too. After a while more sand would settle to the bottom and cover the shells, and over thousands of years the sand and anything in it would gradually turn into stone.

Mr. C: You're doing fine so far, but what happened to the shell itself?

Pupil   (who by now is completely caught up in the process of trying to solve the mystery):

Well, some of the shell would wear away from the sand rubbing against it. This would be like rough sandpaper wearing it down. I think, too, that the shell might be composed of something that dissolves in sea water.

This particular scene, too, might well continue over a longer period of time. The investigation could very easily extend over several days while each of the pupils involved in the outdoor exploration employed a variety of classroom resources, including books, to gather additional information related to a particular discovery or problem under study.

To teach in the manner of a Mr. Catalyst requires skill and experience. For example: How does a teacher set the stage for inquiry? What kinds of questions promote inquiry? What kinds of questions defeat inquiry? How can a teacher start his pupils along a path to self-directed inquiry where the learner poses his own questions?

The intent of inquiry is essentially the act of posing questions which will promote investigation on the part of the learner. The investigative process involves both pupils and teachers, for both are learners. Teachers, in fact, must be able to frame questions for which they themselves do not have the answers. This is a complete break with tradition and a rather frightening one at that. For the traditional questioning process assumes that in order to ask a question the teacher must first have the answer.

Countless inventions and scientific discoveries would never have been made if the initial investigator or inquirer had based his questions only on known answers. An experienced inquirer cultivates the art of posing questions which will lead the learner to discover that which he does not know.

Picture a group of third grade inquirers—explorers—potential discoverers. They have wandered into a field and have come upon a flower that is strange to all, even to the teacher. The ensuing dialogue takes place:

Child: Here's a plant I've never seen before. I wonder what it is.

Teacher: Well, before we try to find out what it is let's see just how much we can learn about it. Do you see any others like this one close by?

Children: Yes, here's one over here. I've found another. I'm standing by one.

Teacher: All right, now what enabled you to pick out these other plants just like this one?

Children: They're the same color. They're about the same size.

Teacher: All right, now let's get even better acquainted with this stranger. Just exactly how tall do these plants grow?

The children measure exact heights and then compute the average height of this particular species. The teacher could then continue the investigation by prompting the children to observe more closely with questions such as: How many petals do you find? How are the leaves positioned on the stem? Draw a quick sketch of the leaf so you have recorded the shape. Is the stem smooth or fuzzy?

Teacher: Let's observe this plant in a slightly different manner. Up to now we have tried to become familiar with its characteristics so we can recognize others like it, and so that we can eventually track it down in one of our flower books. Let's observe now where the plant is growing.

Children: Most of them seem to like the sunny spots.

Teacher: Feel the soil, would you say it is mainly clay or sand?

Children: It feels pretty sandy to me. Yes, and it's pretty rocky around here, too.

So the questioning would continue, and the accumulating evidence mount up to be analyzed, sifted, and refined into basic concepts and broad generalizations concerning the appearance, the characteristics, the growth, the habitat, the requirements of this plant in particular and of plants in general. This is inquiry in an outdoor laboratory situation. The learner is involved *in* and *with* the object of study in its *natural setting*.

Is it possible to motivate children to inquire? By all means. Inquiry is most often triggered by some perplexity on the part of the learner. "I wonder why." "I wonder how." "I wonder what." "I wonder when."

How can a teacher motivate pupils to inquire? A problem or a series of "problem episodes" can be posed which will puzzle, perplex, provoke, and heighten curiousity. Consider the situation in which the teacher confronts the children with a problem. The strategy is for the pupils to initiate inquiry by posing questions to the teacher that can be answered only with a "yes" or "no." This approach forces the learner not only to inquire by observing and searching out relevant data, but more importantly to verbalize his inquiry.

Picture the following: Further along the gully just around one of those intriguing bends the class has come upon a muscular-looking tree, roots exposed, yet still clinging to the wall of the gully. The teacher's lead question designed to promote questions from the children is simply, "What happened here?"

Pupil: Is the tree dead?

Teacher: No.

Pupil: Is this part of the main trunk? (It has the appearance of the trunk because it is covered with a barklike substance.)

Teacher: No.

Pupil: Then are these roots?

Teacher: Yes.
Pupil: Was this part of the tree once under the soil?
Teacher: Yes.
Pupil: What happened to the soil?
Teacher: Rephrase your question, please.
Pupil: Was the soil washed away from the roots?
Teacher: Yes.
Pupil: But these don't look like roots—they're covered with bark.
Teacher: Ask some more questions.
Pupil: When the tree roots were uncovered would they have been smooth?
Teacher: Yes.
Pupil: Could the roots be injured in this condition?
Teacher: Yes.
Pupil: I've got it. Did the tree grow bark over the exposed roots to protect
           them?
Teacher: You've gotten it all right. The answer is, yes.

This particular teaching strategy reverses the usual procedure of teacher asking and pupils answering. The *pupil-inquirers* frame the questions and the teacher simply confirms information with a "yes" or a "no."

In order to pose relevant questions, pupils are forced to come to grips with various essential elements of the object or situation being studied. The learner must synthesize observable data in order to formulate pertinent questions. In this situation pupils are forced to cultivate the art of questioning. This strategy ultimately leads the learner to inquire on his own, independent of the school situation and the teacher. Thus we have the "complete learner," the self-learner.

THE CLUE CHART APPROACH FOR GETTING TO KNOW THE BIRDS

One of the best ways to find birds and to become acquainted with them is to bring the birds to the observer. This can best be accomplished by erecting a feeding station in a spot which has suitable cover such as thick shrubs, berry bushes, blow-downs, or a hedgerow and supplying it regularly with a variety of feed. Most birds prefer a feeder that has good cover nearby so they may approach the feeding area rather cautiously, by easy stages. A week or two may pass before birds are attracted to a new feeding area; do not become discouraged if you have only a few visitors at first. Business will pick up as soon as the bird word gets around. In addition to the steady customers, who in all probability are permanent residents, the feeder will be visited by different species as the seasons change.

Suet will attract quite a few birds. Among those which show a decided preference for this food are chickadees, nuthatches, titmice, brown creepers and

hairy, downy, and red-bellied woodpeckers. The colorful cardinal favors sunflower seeds. Blue jays are the least finicky eaters; they will feed on almost anything. Other foods which can be put out are squash and pumpkin seeds, popcorn, cut-up apples, nutmeats of various kinds and, of course, the old standby, bread and cracker crumbs.

How do youngsters learn about birds? Merely seeing a bird does not guarantee that it will be recognized. The *Clue Chart* is a highly effective technique for teaching children to make discriminating observations; furthermore, it encourages them to record their observations.

A bird perches on a fence post for a minute or two before flying off. In those few moments the children, under the teacher's guidance, ought to look for the following clues. Is the bird robin-size, or larger, or smaller? If he is larger or smaller than a robin, is he crow size, or sparrow size? These will be the three standards of size since most children have a fairly accurate concept of these three common birds. Next, what is or are the predominant color, or colors, and are there any distinctive patterns or markings on our unknown friend? What about his shape in general: tail, slender and long or short and stubby, rounded or crested head, long or short beak? Size, shape, color, and markings will enable the novice to identify many common birds. Picture a hiking group resting by the trailside. A bird alights long enough for them to observe that it is robin-size, has a crest, and is entirely red. It doesn't take long for several children to locate this colorful specimen in one of the standard field guides and determine that they saw a cardinal.

As children gain experience in observing they will learn to make finer discriminations. The main object is to look first at the bird as a whole, and then to look for specific characteristics which will enable the observer to distinguish it from other birds. For example, in addition to noting whether the tail is long or short, one should ask whether the tail feathers are long and pointed, long and rounded, or short and square. In addition to noting whether the beak is long or short, one should ask whether it is thick, slender, or a particular color.

If a bird song is heard, does it rise or fall? Does the song say anything, as do the "peter-peter-peter" of the tufted titmouse, the "teacher-teacher" of the oven bird, the well-known "drink-your-tea" of the towhee, or the "chew-chew, sweet, sweet, chew, chew," of the indigo bunting? Children should first be encouraged to listen carefully and jot down what the song sounds like to them. Different individuals will hear the same song differently. A child will learn to recognize a bird call best by what it sounds like to him—not by what it says in the book. After all, let's be realistic—the birds haven't read the book yet—they don't know what they are supposed to sound like.

Personal observation will add to an individual's knowledge of where to look for birds. We can note the surroundings in which a particular bird is most often found. Is it near the water, along the roadside, in the fields, or in the deep woods? Is the bird sighted most often on or near the ground, midway in the foliage, or always in the very tops of the trees?

In flight does the bird swoop, soar, flutter, dip and dive, fly straight as an arrow or with an up-and-down wavelike motion? Birds can be recognized as accurately by their flight characteristics as an individual can by his walk.

Some of the blocks in the *Clue Chart* are not filled in. It is highly unlikely that on any one day the observer will be fortunate enough to see all of the characteristics of a particular species. In all likelihood, a goodly number of field excursions will be needed before the observer gathers sufficient firsthand information to complete his personal *Clue Chart*.

The discerning teacher soon learns to use prudence and judgment in giving answers to students. The student should be encouraged to gather his own information whenever possible. The learner out-of-doors should be guided to make his own observations, draw his own conclusions, and thus find his own answers to the countless "unknowns" in the natural environment. For instance, it is of little value to the child when the teacher announces that a red-headed woodpecker just flew by. If the child did not see the bird he still has no idea what it looks like. All he knows is that the bird flew past and was sighted by the teacher.

Naturally, every student in the group will not be aware of each bird that happens by. A step in the right direction, however, would be to show the children a picture of the bird that was observed, and to follow up with something on the order of: "What do you want to remember about this bird in order to recognize him?" "How large do you think this bird is?" "What are the main colors?" "How is he marked?" "Sandy, will you read the description aloud for the rest of us?" "Where are we most likely to find this bird—perched

The structure of a *Bird Clue Chart* might look something like this:

SIZE	SHAPE	COLOR OR MARKINGS	LOCATION OR SURROUNDINGS	SONG	FLIGHT PATTERN	NAME
SPARROW	TUFTED HEAD	MOSTLY GRAY WITH RUSTY FLANKS	SEEN IN THE WOODS	WHISTLES "PETER-PETER-PETER"		TUFTED TITMOUSE
ROBIN	CHISEL BEAK	HEAD: ALL RED BACK: BLACK & WHITE BREAST: WHITE	HARDWOOD FOREST	SEEMS TO BE SCOLDING & SAYING "QUEER, QUEER, QUEER"	SWOOPS AS IT FLIES	RED-HEADED WOODPECKER
SMALLER THAN A SPARROW		BLACK CAP & RIB WHITE CHEEK GRAY BACK	SEEN IN THE WOODS, IN THE ORCHARD & IN THE FRONT YARD	SAYS HIS NAME "CHICKADEE DEE-DEE"	FLITS ABOUT A LOT	BLACK-CAPPED CHICKADEE

on a wire, near the ground, in a field, or in the forest?" "Take a good look at the picture once more; then let's keep a sharp lookout, perhaps we'll see him again."

The teacher who employs this approach is helping pupils to develop the kind of observational techniques which will enable them to learn how to recognize unfamiliar specimens. These observational techniques along with the *Clue Chart*

A bird in the hand is worth two in the book.

approach enable the learner to become familiar with hitherto unfamiliar areas of knowledge.

THE DIRECT EXPERIENCE APPROACH IN LEARNING TO RECOGNIZE TREES

Begin with reality—the thing itself. Rather than starting with book knowledge and then going into the field to identify trees from the description in the texts, let us try a new and a more direct approach. Any tree which is unfamiliar will do for a starter. Eventually, we want to find out what this "unknown" tree is called—trees, like families, have names. The ultimate aim is to learn much more than the name, however. Many would-be naturalists are able to rattle off name after name, perhaps even a Latin name or two, but know little more about the tree. They may not know, for example, when the tree flowers, what birds nest in it, the appearance of the fruit, the texture of the bark, the quality of the wood or its use.

The exploratory approach can be readily adapted to this learning task. In practice, it is a "natural." This outdoor teaching technique involves going to the thing itself—the unknown object—and attempting to discover as much as possible about it from firsthand observation. The time of year will make no appreciable difference. This approach works equally well at any season, since it is based upon the learner's ability to examine closely the object about which he wants to learn. During the winter months, of course, the observer must learn to rely on identifying characteristics other than leaves. The color, pattern, and texture of the bark, the shape and color of the buds, the overall configuration of the tree—all are vital observations to make in developing a *Clue Chart* as an aid to recognizing trees.

The teacher, once again, will need to play a key role in guiding children to make discriminating observations. "Let's feel the bark before describing it." "Would you say that it is rough or smooth?" "How would you describe the color of the bark?" "Does it look brown to you, or gray, or greenish?" It doesn't matter how the bark is described in the tree book; if it looks gray to the observer rather than brown, he should remember it as being gray.

One technique which the authors have found to be most effective is to have the students pair off in teams, each team choosing a different tree. They then study the tree for five or ten minutes and record the characteristics that they will want to remember. Their purpose is to note those characteristics that will enable them to distinguish this tree from others. The students then read their descriptions to see if they contain information that is complete, accurate, and sufficiently specific to enable others in the group to recognize the tree. It can readily be seen that this little exercise in perception and expression calls for discriminating observation and accurate description.

The main idea in the "discovery approach" is that the learner asks himself, as he stands before the unknown specimen, "What do I want to remember about this tree in order to be able to recognize others like it?" As each student gathers notes in the field for his own personal *Clue Chart for Trees* he may come up with something on the order of the chart below.

Finding sufficient evidence to fill in each column of the *Clue Chart* may

TREE CLUE CHART

SHAPE	LEAVES	BUDS	BARK	FLOWER	FRUIT	ANY DISTINCTIVE CHARATERISTICS	NAME
LARGE & SPREADING			PEELING WITH - - - MARKS	SMALL GREENISH HANG IN CLUSTERS	TWISTY BEAN 10"-18" LONG	LARGE THORNS GROWING IN CLUSTERS	HONEY LOCUST
LIMBS GNARLED & TWISTED	PINCHED WAIST	IN A CLUSTER & ROUND	DEEPLY RIDGED			ACORN CAP WITH FRINGE	BUR OAK
LIMBS REACH UPWARD	POINTED TIPS	IN A CLUSTER & POINTED	VERTICAL LIGHT & DARK STRIPPING	LONG DROOPING CATTAILS	ACORN	SHALLOW ACORN CAP LONGISH NUT	RED OAK
		LARGE EGG-SHAPED	PEELING SCALY		NUT	SHAGGY BARK	SHAG-BARK HICKORY

require many observations over several seasons. For example, an observer's flower column may be incomplete until he discovers the tree in its flowering stage. Once having completed a *Clue Chart*, however, the learner will have more firsthand knowledge of the trees which he has studied than the person who has gained his information from books alone. Quite often one distinctive characteristic is sufficient to identify a particular tree. Once having developed a *Clue Chart*, the student will readily recognize, even in winter without its leaves, a tree which has opposite budding and branching and whose twigs are square to the touch rather than round, as a blue ash. Even the beginning observer of nature soon learns to recognize the honey locust solely by its distinctive clusters of long thorns.

The teacher's role once again is not to point out and name ten or twenty trees while hiking. It is highly unlikely that students would long remember more than two or three trees learned in this fashion. On the other hand, the teacher's role is to lead pupils to familiarize themselves with these unknown objects by close, firsthand study. This approach to gaining familiarity with unknown subject matter puts the responsibility for learning squarely upon the learner's shoulders—where it should be. Teachers, no matter how inspired, cannot possibly learn for their students, but they can show them how to learn for themselves. In the outdoor classroom students soon learn to rely on their own observations and their own judgments. They look to their teacher not for the answer to everything, but for guidance in thinking.

THE EXPLORATORY APPROACH APPLIED TO THE STUDY OF ROCKS AND MINERALS

The study of rocks and minerals is another subject matter area which lends itself particularly well to the "exploratory" or "discovery" approach to learning in the outdoor classroom. Even first and second grade youngsters can make some basic discoveries about rocks through direct experience. Here is one approach: as they hike along, the teacher instructs the children to search for and collect as many different looking rocks as they can. Before the children become too loaded down with specimens, they are directed to sit in a circle where everyone will have a front row seat. The next step is to see how much can be discovered about the rocks which have been collected. First, the rocks are felt and separated into two piles, those that feel rough to the touch and those that feel smooth. The rocks are then separated into more piles, this time according to color. Next, can any of the rocks be scratched with a fingernail? Those that cannot be scratched are tested with a penny and then with a knife blade.

This initial experience with rocks may take an hour or more without the name of one rock or mineral being mentioned. At this point, names are of secondary importance. Of far greater importance is that children are discovering some of the fundamental properties of rocks. Rocks vary in texture—some rough, others smooth, some hard, others soft—and they vary in the degree of hardness or softness. It will be noted that some rocks are composed of ingredients varying in color. The generalization would be: these rocks must be made of different substances (minerals). This is, of course, a very elementary approach; nonetheless, it is basic to sound learning.

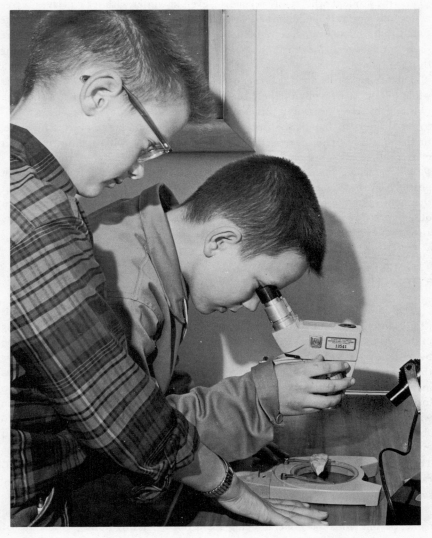

The magic eye of a microscope provides a new look at a common old rock.

Older pupils would want to pursue the investigation much further. "We see layers in this rock; how do you suppose it was formed?" "This specimen has different chunks of material in it; can you tell how it might have been formed?" Discoveries of this sort can lead to insightful discussions pertaining to the types of rocks which are formed under water and those which are formed from molten material and harden deep within the earth's crust. After children have made some of these basic discoveries for themselves it is a good idea to let them examine several samples that demonstrate how rocks are formed and change form. Most young children are familiar with sand, having played in a sandbox or at the beach. They can observe that tiny grains of sand have been cemented together to form stone. In most cases, children can even name the rock correctly. The teacher might continue, "Frequently, sandstone is melted and pressed together to form a new rock called quartzite." "This is a sample of quartzite." A similar "story of change" can be demonstrated with mud or clay changing to shale and finally to slate. Children are fascinated to learn the origin of their schoolroom blackboards. Many modern chalkboards are, of course, synthetic. The "old-fashioned" slate boards are still most serviceable, however.

For children to learn first that rocks are called sedimentary, igneous, or metamorphic is neither necessary or desirable. Nor should the teacher feel that he must wait until his pupils can understand these terms before introducing the study of rocks. It is far more desirable for children to think first of rocks in terms of being water-formed, fire-formed, or changed. Then, when more technical terms are introduced at a higher grade level, they will have greater meaning.

SOLVING PROBLEMS ABOUT A RIVER

A significant learning situation may often develop when one least expects it. To ignore it would be to miss the teachable moment, but to stop and consider it may result in developing an exciting, thought-provoking, on-the-spot lesson in problem solving.

Such a situation might arise spontaneously when a group is hiking along a river. As the group pauses to gaze at the river or to dip their hands in the water, questions are frequently raised. "How deep is this river?" "I wonder how far it is to the other side." "How fast is the water flowing?" To pass on to something else would be easy, but to help the youngsters find some of the answers to their questions would prove to be quite a challenge. If the teacher were to throw these questions back to the children for them to solve, the pupil who wanted to know the depth of the river might reply, "We can measure the depth at the river bank with a stick." But then another member of the group would join in, "But that wouldn't be the depth at all places across the river." However, another suggested solution would not be long in coming—"We could get a boat and lower a

The outdoor laboratory offers many opportunities for measurement problems.

weighted string at many different spots." Soon the children would have the data they would need to determine the depth of the river at various distances from the bank.

The group may think that while they have a boat it would be a relatively simple matter to stretch a string across the river and then measure it. However, this method might prove extremely impractical. The teacher could guide the pupils in their thinking by telling them that there are several ways in which they might solve the problem without leaving this side of the river. Depending somewhat upon the grade level and the ability of the group, they might come up with the "Napoleon Method" or the "Pace-Angle Method."

HOW TO MEASURE THE WIDTH OF A RIVER USING THE PACE-ANGLE METHOD

Procedure:

1. Locate a tree on the other side of the river (A).
2. Place a stick on this side exactly opposite the tree (B).
3. Walk along the shore at right angles to AB. Take 100 paces and at this point place another stick (C).
4. Continue walking along the shore in the same line for another 50 paces. At this point place another stick (D).
5. Turn away from the river at (D), and walk at right angles to DB. When you sight stick C and mark A in a straight line, STOP. This point is (E).
6. DE is then half the distance across the river. Pace this distance. Double this number to get the full distance across the river at AB.

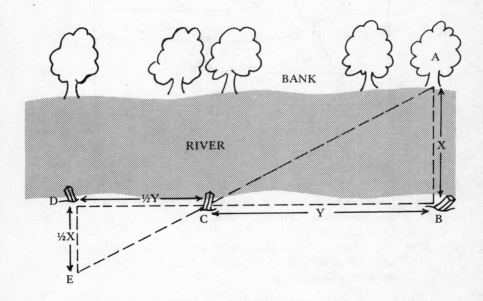

HOW TO MEASURE THE WIDTH OF A RIVER USING THE NAPOLEON METHOD

The "Napoleon Method" is a rather simple procedure for approximating the width of a river. The only equipment needed is a hat or cap with a brim. Lacking this, one may hold his hand palm down, just above the eyes. This method for estimating distances consists of the following three steps:

Step one: Sight under the hat brim or edge of palm to the opposite edge of the

Pace off to determine
distance in feet or yards

Turn Right or Left

river bank (Tree A). Raise or lower the head until a proper line of
sight is drawn.

Step two: Holding the head perfectly still, turn at right angles to the river
            (either direction, up- or down-river; the nature of the terrain may
            determine this). Line up the hat brim or edge of palm with some
            landmark (Tree B).

Step three: The distance from where you stand to the sighted landmark
            approximates the width of the river. Pace it off, and determine the
            distance in feet or yards.

HOW TO CALCULATE VELOCITY OF A RIVER CURRENT

Determining the speed of the river current might prove a bit more difficult.
However, when the children reach the point where they realize that rate of flow
is the same as so many distance units per time unit, the solution is close at hand.
One approach would be to measure off a known distance beside the river bank,
for example, 100 feet. Then one of the students throws a floating object into the
river while another records the length of time it takes to cover the measured
distance. The result of this calculation would be in feet per second. Here the
question may arise, "Is the rate of flow in the middle of the river the same as

that near the bank?" Throwing a floating object at varying distances from the river bank will lead to a solution. Since rate of feet per second may be difficult for the pupils to conceptualize, one youngster may suggest converting it to miles per hour, a rate with which they are more familiar. Thus, another realistic problem involving arithmetic fundamentals arises.

Pupils may ponder the following questions while working on the mathematical calculations: "How many seconds in an hour?" "How far would a floating object be carried in one hour at this rate?" "How many feet in a mile?" "To change over do we multiply or divide?" For example, if the children had determined from their initial trial that the rate of flow was 10 feet per second, the answer when converted would be 6.8 miles per hour. The calculation is as follows:

Feet per min. = 10' x 60 = 600'/minute
Feet per hour = 600' x 60 = 36,000'/hour
Miles per hour = $\dfrac{36,000'}{5,280}$ = 6.8 miles/hr.

USING A FIELD TRIP GUIDE SHEET

Another outdoor teaching technique which ought to be singled out for special attention at this point is the *Field Trip Guidelines* type of instructional aid. The development of such a teaching aid requires considerable forethought on the part of the teacher or trip leader. A preliminary survey of the field trip site is absolutely essential in order to make rough notes on points of interest and subject matter to be covered.

The particular advantage of the *Field Trip Guide Sheet* is that it serves as a ready-made guide to the sequence of the trip. It helps to direct everyone's attention to the same specific points. Each person in the group shares in a common experience. The *Guide Sheet* may (1) pose questions, (2) point out specific items of interest, (3) clarify terminology, and (4) provoke thought and further discussion on the spot. As such it is purely a supplementary instructional aid. The *Guide Sheet* cannot possibly take the place of the teacher. Properly used, however, within its own natural limitations, it serves as a most effective teaching aid.

This instructional device lends itself particularly well to promoting independent investigation on the part of the student. Children will proceed along the trail at their own rates of speed. Some will want to stop longer than others to examine a "find" of particular interest.

There are a few pitfalls to avoid when using the *Field Trip Guide Sheet*. One danger is that some individuals will fall into the trap of using the *Guide Sheet* simply as a check list and follow it so closely that they may be inclined to overlook, or even ignore, an exciting discovery along the way. By the same token, it is possible for the teacher to adhere so closely to the items on the *Guide Sheet* that he may miss a splendid opportunity for capitalizing on the "teachable moment."

The *Guide Sheet*, "A Hike to Ganymede Spring," is merely an example of one form that this instructional aid may take.

This *Guide Sheet*, it will be noted, calls attention to the following:

1. some natural hazards,
2. specific trees and plants to identify,
3. a few pertinent questions to ponder.

Using the *Guide Sheet* is only one phase of the total experience. Upon reaching the spring, for example, the teacher undoubtedly would want to discuss a few of the problems it suggests. Ability to identify trees and plants along the trail could be reinforced by playing several nature games such as, "What Leaf Is This?" "Leaf Relay," "Leaf Matching," etc. Upon returning to the classroom the *Guide Sheet* serves as a record of the learnings experienced on the field trip, and can be used to promote further discussion, reading, and reporting.

A HIKE TO GANYMEDE SPRING

Things to see and things to talk about.

_____ Watch your footing, a steep trail can be treacherous.

_____ Watch for a three-leaved vine that can make you itch.
What is it? _____

_____ What kind of rocks are we treading upon? _____
Pick them up—feel them—take a close look!

Trees and plants to see along the trail. . . Check as you recognize them.

_____ Black Locust
_____ Slippery Elm
_____ Smooth Sumac
_____ Hop Hornbeam
_____ Wild Grape Vine
_____ Virginia Creeper
_____ Hackberry
_____ Box Elder
_____ Linden or Basswood
_____ Shagbark Hickory
_____ Yellow Chestnut Oak
_____ Bur Oak

Take a look at the stone quarry halfway down the slope.

_____ What was this stone used for? _____

_____ Note some of the interesting burls on the Hornbeams.
      What is a burl? _____
      Why does it form? _____

_____ The river:
      In which direction is it flowing? _____

_____ Ganymede Spring:
      What is a spring? _____
      What is the water's temperature? _____

THE SELF-GUIDING TRAIL

Possibilities for developing a variety of self-guiding trails are virtually unlimited. Self-guiding trails can be devised to pique one's curiousity, to develop sensory awareness, to test powers of observation, and to pose problem-solving situations. Trails can be planned so that they may be utilized for teaching, review, and testing. A chief advantage of the self-guiding trail is that the learner may proceed by himself at his own pace, and may develop sensitivities and awareness of phenomena that he might tend to overlook in a group situation.

Perquisite to planning and laying out a self-guiding trail is careful study by the leader to determine the characteristics of a particular site. In this manner the unique natural features (including seasonal occurrences or temporary features) can be used to best advantage in planning trail layout, teaching stations, and so on. Guide sheets for the trail may be in the form of a mimeographed check sheet, small printed booklet, or information on signs along the way. A brief sampling of some of the possibilities for devising a self-guiding trail with appropriate teaching stations follows:

SENSORY AWARENESS TRAIL

Station A —Close your eyes and examine the bark of this tree by touch alone.
          —What descriptive words would you use to describe the texture?
          —Now write another brief description based on your visual impression of the tree.
          —Compare the two descriptions in terms of terminology and vividness of vocabulary.
Station B —Stop for a quiet moment by the brook. Listen. What do you hear?
          —Dip your hand in the water. Does it feel warmer or colder than the air? Can you estimate the temperature of the water?
          —Now check your estimate with the thermometer attached to the chain. What was your margin of error in degrees?
Station C —Examine the leaves on this tree.
          —Sketch the leaf veins.

—Is the leaf simple or compound?

—Is the leaf margin smooth or serrated?

—Touch the underside of the leaf. Is it rough or smooth? What does it feel like to you?

Station D —Crush one of these leaves. Smell it. How would you describe the odor?

—Smell a handful of humus beside the trail. What does it smell like?

—Taste one of the pods on this tree (honey locust). How would you describe the taste sensation?

OBSERVATION TRAIL

Station A —Describe this flower. What does it look like to you?

—How many petals? What color are they?

—How are the leaves arranged on the stem?

—Have any of these flowers gone to seed? Describe the seed.

Station B —Examine this snake skin.

—About how long would you say this snake measured?

—What colors do you see?

—Sketch the pattern.

—How does the topside of the skin differ from the underside?

PROBLEM-SOLVING TRAIL

Station A —Can you figure out what animal has his burrow in this hollow log? What is the evidence?

Station B —Can moss on a tree be relied upon as a direction finder?

—Does moss always indicate the direction north?

—Check ten trees in the area to see if this theory is true.

Station C —If you were lost in the woods and had to live off the land in this area for several days, which plants would you select as a source of food?

As can be seen by the foregoing, outdoor teaching techniques do not differ radically from those which have been regularly employed by teachers over the years. Greater stress is perhaps given to drawing information from the student than to merely informing him with so much empty verbiage. A premium is placed upon the involvement of the learner with concrete experience and

problem solving. The student is encouraged to make his own observations and to draw his own conclusions. These procedures, however, have long been utilized by the master teacher.

The important distinction lies perhaps in the unique instructional setting which the extended classroom affords. Outdoors, teachers and pupils are forced away from the traditional classroom stereotypes and, of necessity, must approach new areas of knowledge as mutual learners. When the teacher ceases to learn along with his pupils he ceases to teach.

SELECTED READINGS

Bale, Robert O. *Conservation for Camp and Classroom*. Minneapolis: Burgess Publishing Company, 1962.

*Blackwood, Paul E. "Outdoor Education and the Discovery Approach to Learning." *Journal of Outdoor Education* 1:6-8, Fall, 1966.

*Brainerd, John W. "Schoolgrounds for Teaching Man's Relationship to Nature." *School Science and Mathematics* 64:428-34, May, 1964.

Hasenstab, Louis D. "Techniques for Outdoor Education." *Youth Leader's Digest*, p. 109, December, 1954.

*Hawkins, Donald and Dennis Vinton. "Environmental Education." *Art Education* 23:49-52, October, 1970.

Hillcourt, William. *Field Book of Nature Activities*. New York: G. P. Putnam's Sons, 1950.

Jenkins, J. E. "Study Unit for Outdoor Education and Conservation." *American Biology Teacher* 24:30-31, January, 1962.

Nickelsburg, Janet. *The Nature Program at Camp*. Minneapolis: Burgess Publishing Company, 1960.

*Roossinck, Esther P. "Arithmetic in the School Camp." *The Arithmetic Teacher* 7:22-25, January, 1960.

*These articles may be found in *Outdoor Education: A Book of Readings* by Hammerman and Hammerman (Minneapolis: Burgess Publishing Company, 1973).

Chapter IV
Learning Experiences
for Outdoor Laboratories

Today's teacher must be capable of designing educational experiences that take place in many different types of learning environments. The out-of-doors is one such setting that can be used effectively by educators in the educational process. The variety of outdoor areas that can be utilized as learning laboratories are illustrated on page 11. Several lists of educational experiences are found in Chapter II and elaborated upon in Chapter III. This chapter contains additional examples of learning activities appropriate for use by teachers in the following "outdoor classrooms."

"JUST BEYOND THE CHALKBOARD"— THE SCHOOLYARD

DEVELOPING AWARENESS

The "100 inch hike" allows children to discover and observe many different "things" found along a length of string 100" long.

SCIENCE

Most school grounds are landscaped to some degree. In many cases plants, trees, and shrubs—both foreign and native—have been added for aesthetic and beautification purposes. These areas may be used by the teacher for:

a) Observing seasonal changes: fall to winter to spring.

Environmental quality is everyone's responsibility. (Courtesy Minneapolis Park and Recreation Board and the Minneapolis Public Schools.)

b) Identification and classification: study of flower parts and functions.
c) Soil studies: texture, temperature, pH, structure.
d) Discussing environmental quality: How do these living things enhance the quality of our schoolyard?

MATHEMATICS

If there is a flagpole or some other post that casts a shadow (this can be simulated with a yardstick), the "shadow-tip" exercise is an excellent problem-solving situation. This experience develops a method of determining direction and time. In developing these understandings, the learner must determine relationships between the earth and the sun, rotation and revolution. An inquiry approach should be utilized in following this procedure:

To find direction, mark the tip of the shadow cast from a pole or stick at least 3 feet high. Wait approximately ten minutes or more, and mark the shadow tip again. A straight line through the two marks is an east-west line. Why? Draw a line from the base of the stick to the east-west line so that it will intersect at a 90° angle. This becomes the "noon" or north-south line.

To find the time of day, proceed as above. Draw a line that is parallel to the east-west line that passes through the base of the stick. This becomes the 6:00

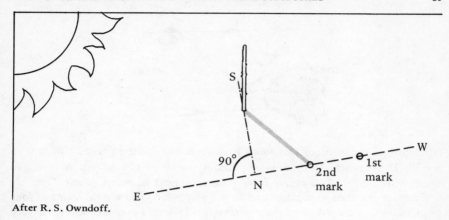

After R. S. Owndoff.

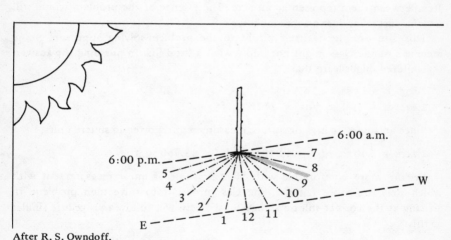

After R. S. Owndoff.

A.M.-P.M. line. Divide the sections between the 6:00 o'clock lines and the "noon" line into sixths to complete the sun clock. The shadow is now the hour hand.

DEVELOPING A REALISTIC CONCEPT OF AN ACRE

Developing a realistic concept of an "acre" is another example of using the school grounds for learnings in mathematics.

A correct verbal answer is very often interpreted as meaning complete understanding of a concept. Children growing up in an urban area can and do memorize tables of measurement in their arithmetic classes without realistic understanding. One typical measure that can be taught effectively and

efficiently in the outdoor classroom is an acre. The question arises, "What is an acre?" The answer, from a book, comes readily: "160 square rods—4,840 square yards—or 43,560 square feet." "Correct, next question, please."

Suppose the class were taken out on the playground and several teams of four boys and girls were asked to place themselves in such a manner that the surface area between them represented an acre. The essence of the problem would still remain—just what does an acre look like?

This situation lends itself nicely to the problem-solving approach. Some members of the class might not know what a "rod" is. In pursuing the answer, the children might learn that:

1 rod = 5½ yds. = 16½ ft.
1 sq. rd. = 30½ sq. yds. = 272½ sq. ft.

Since an acre is an area or surface measurement reported in square units:

1 acre = 160 sq. rds. = 4,840 sq. yds. = 43,560 sq. ft.

Feeling more comfortable with "feet," a unit of linear measurement with which they are more familiar, the class proceeds to solve their problem. In arriving at the correct solution, they most likely will follow a procedure similar to this:

1) If there are 43,560 sq. ft. in an acre, and we know that the area of a rectangle equals the product of the length times the width, how wide will our plot be if we decide to make it 300 ft. in length?
2) A = lw
3) 43,560 sq. ft. = 300 ft. x w
4) $\frac{43,560}{300}$ = w
5) 145.2 ft. = width

The youngsters will undoubtedly want to lay out these measurements with a tape to see how close "their" acres are to the "real" acre. As the class tries out different lengths to the acre, they soon begin to realize that the plot could be not only a rectangle, but a square, or even an area 1 foot wide and 43,560 feet long.

SOCIAL STUDIES

Go on a field trip in the schoolyard. Ask the children to list or name those "things" on the site that man has made from raw materials. Where are these raw materials found? Where is the item made? (For example: bricks [clay] in the building; wooden window frames; iron in the flagpole; glass [sand, limestone, sodium carbonate] in the windows.)

GENERAL

Depending upon the natural "richness" of the school site environment, additional subjects may be studied. One task that every school should undertake is an assessment or inventory of existing study areas, possible learning activities, and development of potential "outdoor laboratories." The following chart represents one possible format for such an inventory:

a) Develop a map or sketch of the school grounds that shows the location of existing buildings, fences, equipment, play areas, vegetation, parking lot, etc.
b) On an overlay sheet (e.g., acetate) or on a separate chart with matching symbols, identify the various areas on the school site that can be used by teachers and students for appropriate learning experiences. For example:

Area	Learning Activities
Fence line	Evidence of animal homes (Science)
Tetherball area	Shadow tip exercise (Mathematics)
Parking lot	Computation of an acre (Mathematics)
Front lawn	Microclimate observations (Science)
Play areas:	Temperature comparisons to various surfaces (Science)
Bare earth	Evidence of erosion: air, water, man (Science)
Grass	Shadow pictures (Art)
Blacktop	

c) On still a different overlay or chart, indicate those developments that would improve the educational potential of the school grounds. For example:

New Study Areas	Learning Activities
One acre arboretum to include:	
Ecological habitats—	Various life cycles plus—
Pond or stream	Water life
Woodland	Plant study
Meadow	Insect study
	Bird study
Special study spots for—	Art, language arts, weather,
(Soil pit)	(Soil study)

Quite often, there are various resource agencies and individuals in the community that (1) would be quite willing to assist in the original planning;

(2) would contribute toward, or donate plants and materials for the new developments. Students should be involved as much as possible in all aspects of such developments. It is through projects similar to this that children formulate basic concepts and understandings relating to managing a quality environment.

"DOWN THE STREET OR ACROSS TOWN"— THE CITY PARK OR A VACANT LOT:

Most communities contain one or more parks that can be used as an "outdoor classroom." If not, there usually are vacant lots or open fields nearby that can serve the same purpose. Quite often, these "barren" areas provide an excellent laboratory for the study of ecological relationships.

The following questions might serve as a guide for exploring a vacant lot or park area:

1. What plants dominate the area? (Don't worry about immediate identification; just describe the plants.)
2. How are the plants distributed over the area? (Sparsely? Abundantly?)
3. What characteristics do these plants possess that enable them to survive at this location?

Improving the environment is one way of contributing to a better society. (Courtesy Minneapolis Park and Recreation Board and the Minneapolis Public Schools.)

4. What kind of root system do these plants have? (How deep?)
5. How many different kinds of plants can you distinguish?
6. What plant-insect associations exist? (Relationship, if any?)
7. Is there any evidence of bird or rodent life?
8. What soil characteristics exist? (Relationship to plants?)

At certain times of the year, a variety of seeds will be found in most vacant lots or parks. A series of lessons might flow from an investigation of how seeds are disseminated.

a) How many different ways do seeds travel? (Based upon observation.)
   (1) Gliders   —maple and pine
   (2) Sailors   —coconut and sedge
   (3) Parachutes   —dandelions
   (4) Hitch-hikers   —pitchfork and burdock
   (5) Explosive   —pea and clematis
   (6) Animal food   —apple and grape
b) Classify seeds as to:
   (1) Vegetable
   (2) Weed
   (3) Grain
   (4) Evergreen garden flower.

Offshoot learnings from the above investigations can lead to a study of how seeds germinate (some will not germinate if left in the cold); or a field trip to a nursery (still another type of outdoor laboratory) to observe which plants are grown and for what purposes.

Adopting a nearby tree (one tree per student) and recording monthly observations can aid in developing the concept of "tree-ness." Some guiding questions are:

a) Where is the tree found? Describe its habitat.
b) What is the general shape of your tree?
c) What is the approximate heighth of the tree?
d) Describe the relationship of your tree to other nearby trees, if any. Are there any similarities? Differences?
e) How do the branches on your tree grow?
f) Record the characteristics of your tree during the four basic seasons of the year. Draw a picture of the leaf, the flower, the fruit.
g) Do you notice any evidence of injury or decay? What might have caused it? How could it have been prevented?
h) What other plants live in or on the tree? (Algae, moss, lichens, fungi.)
i) What animals live in or on your tree? (Birds, insects, other animals.)
j) Can you judge the age of your tree? (The teacher might be able to obtain a tree core with an increment borer.)

After an appropriate period of time for study, the students might compare their findings and then explain the differences in their findings.

If the park is sufficiently large, a novel learning experience is a "Destination Unknown" hike.

The learner, in this activity, uses a compass to find his way into the unknown. All the elements of high adventure are contained in the "Destination Unknown" hike.

To organize the activity, the teacher divides the class into four small hiking groups. Each group will follow a different compass path. The trails are laid out in such a way that they all lead to the same destination. When the hikers start out with their own set of compass directions they have no idea where the trail will lead, or where it will end. The only thing they know for certain is that if they follow the directions carefully they should all finish at the same spot. The overall pattern of directions could look like this.

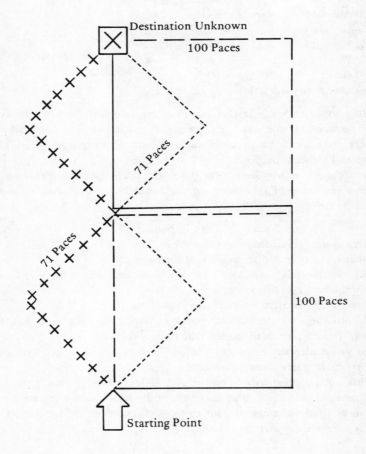

Destination Unknown

100 Paces

71 Paces

71 Paces

100 Paces

Starting Point

Before starting on the trail the students will need to receive instruction on how to use the compass in order to follow a designated set of directions.

PARTS OF THE SILVA COMPASS*

Base—plastic
   Direction of travel arrow
Housing—metal
   Compass needle
   (red-tipped)
   Orienting arrow
   (outlined in black)
   Degrees— 0 - 360

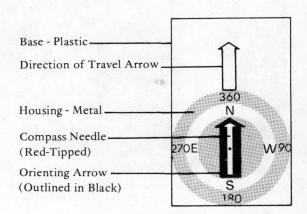

Instructions for using the compass to follow a designated set of directions.

1. Hold the compass by its base and turn the metal housing until the desired degree or direction is lined up with the *direction of travel arrow* in the base.
2. Hold the compass level, with the direction of travel arrow pointing straight ahead, away from you. Turn yourself (not the compass) until the red-tipped compass needle and the black outlined arrow are pointing the same way.
3. You should be facing in the direction you want to go.

There are four changes of direction on the "Destination Unknown" hike, and each group should travel approximately the same distance. The compass directions for each team would look like this.

Team I ———————	Team II - - - - - - - - - - -	Team III - - - - - - - - - -	Team IV XXX
90° 100 paces	360° 100 paces	45° 71 paces	315° 71 paces
360° " "	90° " "	315° " "	45° " "
270° " "	360° " "	45° " "	315° " "
360° " "	270° " "	315° " "	45° " "

Many teachers find the "study plot" exploration a very valuable experience

*The authors are indebted to Silva, Inc., LaPorte, Indiana, for permission to use this illustration.

High adventure lies ahead as young pathfinders work their
way toward "Destination Unknown."

Firsthand experience reinforces learning, whatever the season of the year. (Courtesy Minneapolis Park and Recreation Board and the Minneapolis Public Schools.)

that can be applied to most any outdoor area. The learner explores a particular site or plot to find out what is there and the interrelationships of living things. Through plot studies, comprehension of ecosystems, succession, and land-uses may be related to any of the traditional subject matter areas. Teachers quite often utilize activities in the plot study as a means for developing the basic process skills of observation, inference, communication, classification, computation, measurement, time/space relationships, and prediction.

"A SHORT BUS TRIP" TO .... A STATE PARK, NATIONAL FOREST, OR NATIONAL PARK:

Depending upon the exact location of one's school, there may or may not be several large "outdoor classrooms" within a short bus ride in the form of a park or forest under the supervision and maintenance of a county, state, or federal agency. In addition to the previously described activities, these areas might offer opportunities for the exploration of:

1. A stump or fallen tree.
   a) How did it fall or how was it felled?
   b) Can you establish how long ago the tree was cut down?
   c) How old was the tree when it was cut down?
   d) Was it cut down because of injury? Fire?
   e) What is the tree's diameter? Circumference?
   f) What things live on the stump/log now? Effect?
   g) What nonliving things are affecting the stump/log?
   h) What changes do you think have occurred or will happen in the environment now that the tree has fallen?
   i) Develop a diagram illustrating the energy cycle surrounding your stump/log.
   j) Explain the value of a stump/fallen tree in a forest.
   k) Why is it important not to tear the stump/tree apart?
   l) Communicate your feelings about this encounter with a stump/fallen tree in one or more of the following ways:
      (1) Written form (the teacher might wish to use haiku or cinquain).
      (2) Sketch the stump/tree (charcoal, water colors, ink).
      (3) Photographs
2. Layers of forest life: To the untrained eye a forest sometimes appears to be merely a disorganized collection of plants and trees. Closer inspection will reveal various patterns or layers. Animals also live in this "apartment house" of the plant kingdom. Some animals remain in just one layer of the forest for their entire life; others move about freely. The following table may be used to collect data about life in a forest.

Forest Layer or Floor	Which Plants Are Found?	Which Animals Are Found?
Canopy/Penthouse		
Understory/Top Floors		
Shrub Layer/Middle Floors		
Herb Layer/Lower Floors		
Forest Floor/Lobby		
Under the Ground/ Basement		

Some additional investigations, associated with study of a forest, are:

a) Comparing temperatures: Place at least four thermometers in various zones of the forest and in a nearby open field. (First make sure the thermometers are working properly by placing them all in the same location and see if they all read the same.) Record the temperatures on an overcast day . . . a cloudy day . . . a clear day. Are there any differences? Why?

b) Food chains: From your observations, can you determine what feeds upon what? Diagram your findings with connecting arrows. For example:

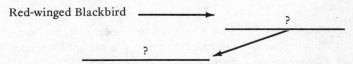

Red-winged Blackbird

?

?

c) Ecological relationships: Summarize the interrelationships of this community with the assistance of the following guide questions:

(1) What producers are in the community? Are these producers rare or abundant?

(2) Which group contributes the most to food production?

(3) Are there layers of producers? What is their relationship?

(4) Which consumers are in the community? What are their relationships?

(5) Is there any evidence of "predator-prey" or "parasite-host" relationships?

SPECIAL AREAS

Many schools are located in areas where there are opportunities to take field trips to "unusual" types of "learning environments." Each one of these examples offers unique learning possibilities and the use of an inquiry approach. A field trip to a farm might enable urban dwellers, especially, to gain some insights into the complex aspects of operating a farm and the interdependence of the farmer and the city dweller.

a) How large is the farm?

b) How far from our school is the farm?

c) What does the farmer grow or raise on his land?

d) Do any animals live on the farm? What kind? How many?

e) Is the farmer troubled by predators or pests? How does he control them?

f) When does the farmer harvest what he grows?

g) Where does he sell his products? How much does he receive for his products on a unit basis?

h) What kinds of assistance (machinery and services) does the farmer receive in order to help him do his job?

i) Does the farmer apply any conservation practices? Which ones and why?

j) How does the work of the farmer help us?

k) How has the way in which the farmer has done his job changed over the past twenty years?

l) What types of fertilizers are used, if any? How much is used? What is the cost? How does it influence the growth of crops?

A lumber mill is another fascinating place to visit. The number of different operations involved in processing the "raw" saw log to finished pieces of lumber is a real "eye-opener" for teachers and pupils, alike. The following questions may serve as a guide to what can be learned on a field trip to an operating lumber mill:

a) What kinds of trees are here and where did they come from?

b) What happens to a tree from the time it is cut until it reaches the mill?

c) Why are the logs separated?

d) Why are the logs kept moist?

e) Why is there a pond? How many logs are in the pond?

f) Who has one of the most important jobs in the mill? Why?

g) How is the lumber transported from the mill? Where?

h) What is the cost of the lumber at this mill?

i) What effect does weather have upon the timber industry?

j) What is being done to replace the trees that are harvested?

A novel problem-solving exercise during a trip to a lumber mill, a tree farm, or a forest is to estimate the number of board feet in a tree (or log). The first step is to calculate the height and diameter of the tree as follows:

The Biltmore stick with a Merritt rule on the reverse side is a handy teaching aid for determining the diameter and height of trees. This instructional tool is easily constructed from a straight piece of wood 30 inches long, 1½ inches wide, ½ inch thick, and beveled on one edge.

The Biltmore stick is graduated along the unbeveled edge as follows:

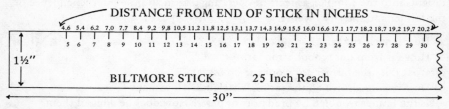

The Merritt rule gradations for the reverse side of the stick are as follows:

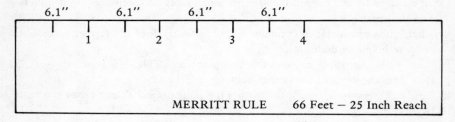

DETERMINING HEIGHT

Each gradation of 6.1 inches on the Merritt rule represents one 16-foot log. To calculate the number of 16-foot log lengths in standing timber:

1. Take a position 66 feet from the base of the tree at approximately the same elevation as the tree base. The stick should be held vertically at a distance of 25 inches from your eye.
2. Sight over the zero end of the stick so that it is in line with the upper limit of usable timber.
3. Without moving the stick or your head, sight along the rule to the base of the tree (12 to 16 inches above ground level is about right). Read directly from the rule the number of 16-foot logs or fractions of logs in the tree.

FIGURING DIAMETER

The Biltmore stick is used for calculating diameter of standing timber. Follow the steps outlined below:

1. The stick is held horizontally, 25 inches from the eyes with the beveled edge against the tree. Diameter measurements are taken at chest height or 4½ feet from ground level.
2. The zero end of the stick should be in line with the left edge of the tree trunk. Holding your head still, sight over the stick to the right-hand edge of the trunk.

A COMPOSITE VOLUME (BOARD FEET) TABLE

Three Diameter (inches)	Number of 16-foot logs				
	½	1	1½	2	. . . .
10	21	39	54	68	
16	59	105	147	180	
20	92	170	236	295	Douglas Fir
26	158	300	410	510	$35.00/1000 Bd. Ft.
30	220	410	550	685	
36	333	600	820	1010	
40	415	745	1010	1250	

3. The diameter is read directly from the stick at the point where your line of vision meets the right-hand edge of the tree.

Then, knowing the type of tree, refer to specially prepared charts that indicate the number of board feet. If the current market price/board foot for that particular kind of wood is known, it is only a simple calculation to determine the value of that tree.

Example: A student estimates that a certain tree will yield 1½ - 16' logs. The estimated diameter of the tree at chest height is 36". At the rate shown in the table on page 77, what is the estimated value of that particular tree?

Rate: $35.00 divided by 1000 equals 3½¢ per bd. ft.
Value: 820 bd. ft. x 3½¢ equals $287.00

Youngsters frequently fish in recreation areas unaware that many of the fish they catch are raised in a fish hatchery. Many states maintain fish hatcheries and welcome educational groups to tour their facilities. As a result of observing, reading display materials, and talking with the guide, the following questions might be answered:

a) What type of fish are raised at this hatchery?
b) What are the troughs for? Where do the eggs come from? How long do they take to hatch?
c) How are the fish cared for in the hatchery? What are some of the problems in raising fish to a catchable size?
d) What effect does the water temperature have upon the length of the incubation period and the rate of growth?
e) How many fish are raised in one year?
f) What happens after the fish hatch?
g) How much food do the fish eat?
h) How are the fish moved to the ponds?
i) What are the different methods of planting fish?
j) How are the fish transported to the planting areas?
k) How much does it cost to raise an 8" fish? Where does the money come from?
l) How many fish are caught per year? How many fishing licenses are sold in your state per year?
m) What laws does your state have to protect fish? Who enforces these regulations?
n) What are some safety rules to follow when fishing?

Many communities have an "old" or "historic" cemetery nearby that can prove to be very educational by revealing much information about the culture of the people who lived there earlier. Recognizing the fact that burial grounds have always been considered "sacred" by man, visitors should treat a cemetery with respect and care. Permission should be sought, if possible, before making a visit with a large group. Small investigating teams may prove to work very effectively in seeking answers to the following guiding questions:

a) When was the cemetery founded?
b) Who was the first person buried? When? What was his age at time of death?
c) How long has it been since someone was buried in the cemetery?
d) What kinds of markers are used on the graves? Are these materials local to the area? Transported from elsewhere?
e) Can the history or family tree of certain families be traced from the grave markers?
f) How many different nationalities or countries are represented within the cemetery?
g) What was the average life span of people in this community?
h) Is there any evidence of plagues, epidemics, or wars?
i) Over the years, did any changes in designs or shapes of markers, or types of markers, or epitaphs take place?
j) Are all the inscriptions visible? What kinds of stones show weathering? (Making rubbings of inscriptions on gravestones might be an interesting activity.)
k) Do the graves all face the same direction? Why?
l) Who lived longer in this community, men or women?
m) Can the economic status of a family be determined in any manner?
n) What feelings do you have about those people who are buried in this cemetery?

Now that approximately 74 per cent of the population in the U.S.A. live on 2 per cent of the land, man has become very concerned about the quality of his total environment from the inner city to wilderness areas. One result of space exploration has been to cause man to realize that his life-space and natural resources are finite . . . that we are all truly passengers on this spaceship called Earth.

Urban areas, in particular, are plagued with complicated environmental quality problems such as air, water, and noise pollution; transportation congestion; lack of decent housing and community facilities; lack of recreational and open land; and inadequate water supplies and waste disposal systems. The urban community, itself, is an ideal laboratory for the study of urban problems and potential solutions. Youngsters may experience many kinds of "environmental encounters" through investigations conducted in the city. For example:

a) Visit the Air Pollution Control District Office for your city or area. (If possible, take photographs from the same viewing spot on a clear day and a smoggy day.)

   (1) How do they determine (measure) the quality of the air? (Amount and types of pollutants?)

   (2) What are the sources of these pollutants?

   (3) How does the quality of air vary during the day? Week? Month?

   (4) What are the effects of air pollution upon people? Plants? Man-made structures?

   (5) What influence do weather and topography have upon air pollution in your area?

   (6) What is the financial cost of air pollution per person per year?

   (7) What is being done to control air pollution in your area? By which agencies? How? Cost? Effectiveness?

b) Identify major traffic intersections or arteries near your school. Assign teams of students to gather the following data at various times during the day.

   (1) How many vehicles pass this point in one hour?

   (2) How many of these vehicles carry one passenger? Two? Three? Four or more?

   (3) How much noise is there at this intersection? (If possible, try to measure with a *"sound-level" meter.*)

Air pollution, house pollution and congestion. Environmental encounters may lead to better solutions.

(4) Could you smell any fumes from the vehicles?

(5) In your opinion, can this intersection/street carry this amount of traffic satisfactorily?

(6) Visit the office of the "Director of Transportation" to find out what plans are being developed to handle transportation of people in your community in the years ahead.

c) Visit your community's waste disposal plant in order to determine how it handles and disposes of municipal wastes.

(1) Is the garbage and trash dumped? Buried? Burned? Or what? Are there any benefits derived from these processes?

(2) Are the waste materials sorted in any manner? If so, how? Are these sorted materials recycled? Does this process save any money?

(3) Are there market places readily available for recyclable materials?

d) Plan a visit with the "Director of Recreation and Parks" or "City Planner" to gather the following information about "open space" available to your city. (If possible, take an aerial field trip and actually view the open space of your community.)

(1) How many acres of permanent open space (e.g., military reservations; wildlife refuges; watershed lands; and city, county, state, or national parks) are available within a one-hour drive? One-half day drive? One-day drive of your neighborhood?

(2) Does your community (county, region, or state) have any policies regarding open space and recreation lands for the public? If so, how many acres of public recreation open space do they recommend for 1,000 population?

(3) Have any studies been conducted to determine the recreation needs of the people in your area? (e.g., hiking, camping, boating, fishing, horseback riding, etc.) Is there sufficient space and facilities to meet these needs?

(4) Are there any plans on the "drawing board" for future needs . . . for the year 2000?

SUMMARY

It is only one's own imagination that limits the "what" and "where" of teaching in the out-of-doors. Man's outdoor environment: a crack in the pavement, a roof-top garden, a city dump, a botanical garden, a mountain forest, or a meadow pond contain numerous learning opportunities that span the total school curriculum. The teacher who fails to develop the skills and techniques necessary to utilize the outdoor laboratory as one of many instructional environments available to his students is limiting the richness of learning opportunities for his class.

SELECTED READINGS

American Camping Association. *Conservation of the Camp Site.* Bradford Woods, Martinsville, Ind., 1960.

Association of Classroom Teachers. *Man and His Environment.* Washington, D.C.: National Education Association, 1970.

Association for Outdoor Education. *Teaching Conservation and Natural Science in the Outdoors.* Sacramento, Calif.: State Department of Conservation, 1964.

Bale, Robert O. *Conservation for Camp and Classroom.* Minneapolis: Burgess Publishing Company, 1962.

Danner, Katherine S., and Marsha A. Reid. *A Manual for Study Plot Exploration.* Bloomington, Ind.: P.O. Box 1336, 1971.

Gray, Alice. "Hunting Pond Insects." *Nature and Science* 2:6-7, July, 1965.

Hug, John, and Phyllis Wilson. *Curriculum Enrichment—Outdoors.* New York: Harper & Row Publishers, 1966.

Marsh, Norman F. *Outdoor Education on Your School Grounds.* Sacramento, Calif.: The Resources Agency, Office of Conservation Education, 1968.

Milliken, Margaret, et al. *Field Study Manual for Outdoor Learning.* Minneapolis: Burgess Publishing Company, 1968.

Nickelsburg, Janet. *Field Trips.* Minneapolis: Burgess Publishing Company, 1964.

Pringle, Laurence. "How to Explore a Pond." *Nature and Science* 2:3-5, July, 1965.

Rillo, Thomas J. "School Grounds Provide Opportunities for Outdoor Teaching." *Illinois Journal of Education* 8:10-12, September, 1967.

St. Regis Paper Company. "The Life of the Forest." Pamphlet, 1969.

Science Curriculum Improvement Study. *Environments.* Berkeley, Calif.: University of California, 1968.

Soil Conservation Service. *The Community School Site: A Laboratory for Learning.* Portland, Ore.: U.S. Department of Agriculture, 1970.

Special Issue, "Exploring a Forest." *Nature and Science* 3(17):June 27, 1966.

Swan, Malcolm D., ed. *Tips and Tricks in Outdoor Education.* Danville, Ill.: Interstate Printers and Publishers, 1970.

U.S. Forest Service. *Conservation Tools for Educators.* Portland, Ore.: U.S. Department of Agriculture, 1968.

Van Matre, Steve. *Acclimatization: A Sensory Approach to Ecological Involvement.* Bradford Woods, Martinsville, Ind.: American Camping Association, 1972.

Vessel, Matthew F., and Arnold G. Applegarth. *Experiences With Living Things.* Palo Alto, Calif.: Fearon Publishers.

Weaver, Richard L. *Manual for Outdoor Laboratories.* Danville, Ill.: Interstate Printers and Publishers, 1959.

Chapter V
Resident Outdoor
School Programs

The resident outdoor school, a program in which a teacher and his pupils live and learn for several days in an outdoor setting pursuing a program of activities related to the school curriculum, is considered to be one of the most "complete" outdoor education experiences. Recognizing the fact that local circumstances and state laws may prescribe specific procedures, resident programs occur under a variety of conditions and may be planned and executed under many different organizational patterns. Some of the unique values of a resident program are highlighted in this chapter along with a description of some basic patterns of program organization and administration.

VALUES OF RESIDENT OUTDOOR EDUCATION

In the total-living situation of the outdoor school setting there are numerous gains, many of which cannot be measured in terms of tangible results. The teacher, in addition to directing the learning activities, is eating three meals a day with his pupils, relaxing with them, helping put them to bed—in a word, *living* with them. Furthermore, the total-living situation enables the classroom teacher to observe his pupils under a variety of conditions in which he would not ordinarily see them. Under these circumstances an entirely new pupil-teacher relationship is bound to be established. Deeper understanding and mutual appreciation are some of the positive outcomes.

TEACHERS AND PUPILS GAIN

For the class, the resident outdoor education experience provides a culmi-
nating activity toward which pupils can work. Another positive value is the
cohesiveness and unity of spirit that results when individuals are pursuing a
common goal.

In this twenty-four-hour-a-day experience children are provided the opportunity to develop a certain amount of independence and self-reliance in assuming
responsibility for their own well-being. They have the opportunity to carry out
various tasks for the successful maintenance of the outdoor school community.
When tables in the dining hall need to be set, for example, or when the buildings
need cleaning, the pupils decide just what needs to be done and how they are
going to go about carrying out the task. Children have an opportunity to assume
real responsibility. Mother is not along to make the bed or clean the room; these
tasks fall to the pupils. They are responsible not only to themselves but to one
another for the well-being and smooth functioning of the total group. The

Pupils explore and discover in the extended classroom.

Now where should I put the knife?

day-in, day-out, close contact with others serves to rub off the rough edges of personality, and provides the setting for learning to plan and work cooperatively with one's peers.

Subject matter which may heretofore have been dull, uninteresting, and lacking in real meaning in the highly verbal setting of the schoolroom takes on new luster when studied firsthand. Children realize that they are involved in a compelling, natural learning situation when they describe outdoor education as "getting close to what we want to learn about," and "seeing what we've always read about."

PARENTS AND COMMUNITY GAIN

The community gains to the extent that more responsible young citizens are developed. Parents, when asked if they had observed any changes in their children following the resident outdoor education experience, responded in the following manner:

"He seems to be more responsible and takes more interest in home duties."
"He's made his bed and cleaned his room each day without being told."
"He has learned how to earn money and do things for himself."
"More independent. Has an interest in much wider and varied fields."

PATTERNS OF ORGANIZATION

A review of organizational patterns reveals a wide range of program planning, staffing, and financial practices and arrangements. There just isn't any one best way in which to conduct a resident outdoor school. Many alternatives are available to the individual school, district, or county office that wishes to develop a resident program. This section describes three basic models.

I. *TEACHER-PUPIL PLANNED*

In this pattern the major effort is made by the classroom teacher and his pupils with the assistance of parents, administrators, and resource people. If the most significant program of study activities is to be designed and the maximum achievement of educational goals are to be obtained, two keys to planning are:

1. Each class should develop its own "tailor-made" program of learning activities so that their experiences in the outdoor school complement their curriculum in the "indoor" school.
2. Each classroom teacher should coordinate the entire sequence—organization, implementation, and evaluation—for his own class.

Teacher Planning

The most logical starting point is for a teacher to clarify the general educational goals and to identify the curriculum objectives he plans to strive toward. These, of necessity, will vary from grade level to grade level, and from school district to school district. One such list, from an upper elementary grade, might read as follows:

   I. To complement the subject matter areas and the objectives of education through direct experience. (These objectives and subject matter areas are elaborated upon in Chapter Two.)
   II. To develop a realization of self.
     A. Self-discovery of individuality and worth.
     B. Realization of value of growth through "giving of one's self."
   III. To develop understanding and appreciation of the out-of-doors.
     A. Realizing relationship of self to cosmos.
     B. Realizing the value of balance in nature.
     C. Recognizing interdependence of plants and animals.
     D. Recognizing man's relationship to the quality of his environment.
   IV. To develop a sense of physical well-being.
     A. Understanding of practices in healthful living.
     B. Realization that the body is an instrument of expression.

V. To develop desirable human relationships and sound social attitudes, values, and concepts.
   A. Accepting and sharing responsibility.
   B. Getting along with others.
   C. Understanding of and appreciation for group living and group planning.
   D. Accepting the individuality of each person.

During the formulation of these goals and objectives, the classroom teacher should consult with the school administrators, curriculum consultants, and special resource people with whom he may be working at the outdoor school.

Preparation With Parents

Very early in the planning stages, preferably before actual preparation is started with the children, an orientation meeting for parents should be held. At such a session, the parents should become acquainted with the purposes and scope of the resident outdoor school. The general nature of the study activities should be outlined along with plans providing for the health, safety, and welfare of the children. The financial share for the parents, if any, should be explained along with the overall cost of the program. Although it is desirable for the entire class to participate, no child should be required to go. In cases of insufficient family funds, the administrator should make every effort through the PTA or some other source to insure that every youngster who is physically able participates.

Parents should be allowed ample time to raise questions about the program, in order to have the clearest understanding possible. This is especially important if it is the initial experience for the school. Quite often, the administrator finds it valuable to include parent representation on the outdoor education policy-making committee. If the site isn't too far from the community an open house at the facility will prove effective.

Planning With Children

The educational benefits of the resident outdoor school begin long before the pupils reach the site. Even though specialists and a resident staff might make all the arrangements in some programs, much is to be gained by the class that develops its own plans in a logical manner. These planning sessions are handled by the teacher as part of the regular school day in the classroom.

After being informed about their opportunity to attend the outdoor school, the class might develop plans as follows (excerpt from the classroom teacher's planning book):

April 9 (11:00-11:40 A.M.) Discussion of Problems.
   I. Why are we going to the outdoor school?

A. We can do things we can't do in the classroom.

B. We can learn through experience, so we'll remember longer.

C. We can "get close" to what we want to learn more about (weather, stars, geology, etc.)

D. We can see things we've read about.

E. We can learn to know each other better.

F. We will have a new experience in being away from home.

G. We can learn to take care of ourselves, be independent.

H. We can help others, cooperate.

II. What will we do? and when? (Program and schedule).

III. What is at the outdoor school? (Facilities and vicinity).

IV. What will we eat? (Menu planning).

April 10 (1:15-3:00 P.M.) Begin discussion about the menu (Start of nutrition unit).

Discuss things to consider in planning a menu.

A. Nutritional value and what makes a balanced diet.

B. Well-liked foods.

C. Religious beliefs.

D. Cost (amount, season, brand, store).

E. Storage facilities at the outdoor school.

F. Transportation.

G. Preparation (time involved).

H. Assign: allergy list for those concerned. Comparative cost survey of grocery store; noting various brands.

Following the teacher-pupil planning procedure above, the class over a three-week period worked on questions and problems such as:

1. What can we best learn at the outdoor school?
2. What shall we have for evening snacks?
3. How shall we organize ourselves into
   a) Study groups?
   b) Cabin groups?
   c) Flag-raising groups?
   d) Store, post office, and bank groups?
   e) Weather-recording groups?
4. What clothes do we need to take?
5. What will we do for evening programs?

When plans are developed in this manner, it is difficult to predict the thousand and one "teachable moments" that will arise. All areas of the curriculum will be touched upon without the labels of history, language arts, mathematics, and science. The teacher does not necessarily have to conduct all

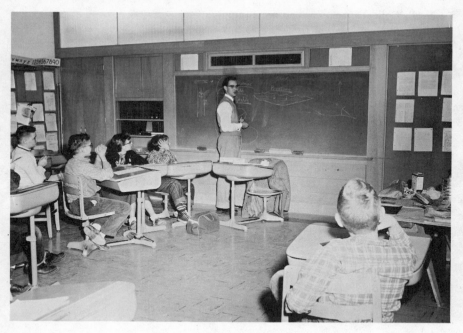

Planning begins in the classroom.

the planning sessions. Student chairmen should assume leadership responsibilities whenever possible; whether it be for a small group or the entire class.

Curriculum consultants or specialists might assist the children in their planning and organization. The music person might help with the preparation of evening programs. The recreation or physical education specialist could teach the children to call their own square dances and assist with their planning of a skit night or a talent show. Other community resource persons might be involved as the classroom teacher saw fit.

It will prove beneficial to the program if the class experiences a few short trips to an outdoor area before going to the resident school. Unless children have had some prior experience in "seeing, listening, tasting, touching, and smelling," two or three days might pass at the outdoor school before they really begin to focus upon the objects of their study activities.

The results of student planning are often startling in that they approach what an adult group might plan. The following outline represents the result of discussions centered around the topic: "What we want to learn and hope to do."

I. Flowers and Seeds
  A. Go on a hike to find specimens.

  B. Collect specimens and press them.
  C. Sketch different flowers.
  D. Learn to tell a wild flower from a garden flower.
  E. Learn to tell flowers from weeds.
  F. Identify seeds and flowers in collections.
  G. Learn some common names and scientific names.
  H. Plant seeds and watch them grow.
  I. Make a "wild flower diary."
II. Water Plants and Animals
  A. Watch for animals and identify them.
  B. Get to know different kinds of water plants and animals.
  C. Look for frog eggs and other stages of growth of frogs.
  D. Make a terrarium and put animals in it.
  E. Collect specimens of water plants.
  F. Magnify smaller specimens.
III. Measuring
  A. Measure an acre, mile, block, yard, etc.
  B. Measure cabins and other buildings.
  C. Go on "bee-line" compass hike.
  D. Estimate your walking speed.
  E. Plot a map.
IV. Trees
  A. Learn 15-20 different trees.
  B. Count rings for age.
  C. Collect wood samples.
  D. Wax or spatter leaves for collections.
  E. Ask man in fire tower about trees.
  F. Make a scrapbook.
V. Rocks and Fossils
  A. Hike for specimens.
  B. Start a collection.
  C. Identify types of rocks.
  D. Identify fossils.
  E. Look for history of area in rocks.
VI. Insects and Small Plants
  A. Collect different kinds of small plants.
  B. Compare sizes of plants.
  C. Where do certain types of plants grow best? Why?
  D. Experiment with types of soil using plants.
  E. Look for insects; put a collection in a case; identify them.
VII. Conservation

    A. Plant seedlings in burned area.

    B. Have forest ranger explain fire fighting equipment.

This model is usually implemented when only a few classes from one or two schools take part in a program and there is no centrally coordinated program at a higher level, i.e., county or region. The site is probably leased or rented for the required number of weeks. The classroom teachers assume the responsibility for completing the arrangements for transportation, medical care, site selection, and finances.

II. ADMINISTRATOR-TEACHER PLANNED

A second model is one in which the basic arrangements (e.g., securing the site, menu planning, food preparation, transportation, and a master program plan) are made by an administrator who usually serves as the on-site director or "coordinator of outdoor education." Although a preplanned calendar of activities and events has been arranged by the outdoor school director, the individual teacher may request that other themes or topics, more relevant to his class, be substituted. In this pattern, the classroom teacher often works closely with the director and his staff in handling instructional responsibilities in the field. If more than one class is at the center at the same time, it is quite possible that no two instructional programs for the week will be the same.

The amount of planning and preparation by the teacher with the pupils and parents is dependent upon how much the individual teacher chooses to take upon himself. Quite often the coordinator conducts one orientation meeting, for the parents of all the children who might attend that season. The classroom teacher might be provided with a manual that recommends various pre-site activities that can be done in the classroom.

When this model is found in operation, it is usually with an outdoor school that is in session for several weeks in the fall and in the spring. Many times, only the on-site administrator is a full-time educator since the resident staff and resource people are seasonal employees. In order to keep the cost per pupil/day at a minimum, three or more classes may occupy the site at the same time. The master calendar of activities for the week might appear as on page 92.

III. ADMINISTRATOR-STAFF PLANNED

Many programs consisting of several school districts, a county-wide system, or a regional area operate for the entire school year and are administered so that all the programs and arrangements are handled by a centralized resident staff. Very few modifications, if any, are allowed in the program of learning experiences. The classroom teacher is usually an observer with occasional opportunities to meet with his pupils for planning or review purposes.

ADMINISTRATOR-TEACHER PLANNED PROGRAM SCHEDULE
GENERAL CURRICULUM FORMAT

	Monday	Tuesday	Wednesday	Thursday	Friday
Morning	Classes arrive Settle into cabins or dormitories Orientation to Outdoor School Site	Class #1–Field Math: measurements #2–Hike to Fire Lookout Tower #3–Trace water Supply for camp #4–Geology Hike	Class #1–Plot Study: Hillside #2–Explore Old Mill Road (All-day hike) #3–Use of Compass Layout Courses #4–Study of Redwood Forest	Class #1–Tide Pool Study #2–Tide Pool Study #3–Conservation Project: Plant Seedlings #4–Weather Study: Use of Instruments	Class #1–Conservation Project: Erosion Control #2–Creative Expression Time: Highlight of Week #3–Recycle project w/camp's garbage dump #4–Problem: Estimate Daily Water Use at Camp
Afternoon	Class #1–Redwood Community #2–Map & Compass Problems #3–Destination Unknown Hike #4–Hike to the Lumber Mill	#1–Field Math: mapping with plane table #2–Explore stream #3–Pond Study: Ecological Relationships #4–Soil Study: Use of Test Kit	#1–Plot Study: Hillside #2–Visit Lumber Mill #3–Orienteering Competition #4–Use of Compass	#1–Beach Study #2–Visit Village Cemetery #3–Photography Projects #4–Free Choice/ Special Interests	Group Depart
Evening	All Classes Evening Campfire Early history of area songs. Folk dancing	#1–Pine Cone Sculpture #2–Campfire-stories #3–Star Study #4–Night Hike: Animal Sounds	#1–ABC Scavenger Hunt #2–Compass Course Treasure Hunt #3–Arts & Crafts #4–Star Study	All Classes Evening Campfire Group Skits Songs Stories	

ADMINISTRATOR–STAFF PLANNED PROGRAM SCHEDULE
SCIENCE-CENTERED CURRICULUM FORMAT

	Monday	Tuesday	Wednesday	Thursday	Friday
Morning	Class arrive Settle into cabins or dormitories Orientation to Outdoor School Site	Class #1–Tide Pool Study #2–Conservation Project #3–Geology Trail #4–Nature Arts & Crafts	Class #1–Conservation Project #2–Tide Pool Study #3–Nature Arts & Crafts #4–Geology Trail	Class #1–Geology Trail #2–Nature Arts & Crafts #3–Tide Pool Study #4–Conservation Project	Class #1–Nature Arts & Crafts #2–Geology Trail #3–Conservation Project #4–Tide Pool Study
Afternoon	Class #1–Redwood Community #2–Map & Compass #3–Plot Study: Chaparral Habitat #4–Beach Study	#1–Beach Study #2–Redwood Community #3–Map & Compass #4–Plot Study: Chaparral Habitat	#1–Plot Study: Chaparral Habitat #2–Beach Study #3–Redwood Community #4–Map & Compass	#1–Map & Compass #2–Plot Study: Chaparral Habitat #3–Beach Study #4–Redwood Community	Classes Depart
Evening	All Classes Evening Campfire Early History of Area Singing Story Study	All Classes Library Period Demonstration of Weather Instruments Square Dancing Star Study	All Classes Film: Conservation Evening Campfire Star Study	All Classes Evening Campfire Group Skits Songs Stories	

A teacher's guide or manual outlines the responsibilities of the outdoor school staff, parents, principals, and classroom teachers in great detail. Suggested pre- and post-site activities are recommended to the teacher. The school unit may sponsor a special training and orientation weekend in the fall for all the classroom teachers who will be attending the outdoor school that year.

Several classes (four or more) might attend at the same time and participate in the program of activities on a staggered basis. The children are sometimes mixed with those from other classes or schools in forming study teams, eating or cabin groups. Due to the large numbers at the site at any one time, the daily routine tends to become structured and highly organized. The weekly block plan on page 93 illustrates a science-centered outdoor school curriculum.

LOGISTICAL ARRANGEMENTS COMMON TO ALL THREE MODELS

SITE AND FACILITY

The selection of the site and facilities utilized by the school unit does not follow any "rule-of-thumb." Some schools own their resident outdoor education center as a result of purchase or donation of property. Many others, however, lease or rent various types of sites: federal and state facilities; agency or church camps; or private facilities. In any event, these accommodations are adequate in that they provide:

a) Housing units (dormitories, cabins, tents)
b) Dining hall and kitchen facilities
c) Restroom and shower facilities
d) Multipurpose hall or recreation building
e) Staff quarters
f) Infirmary or first aid room.

Whether the facility is owned or rented, it should be approved by the local health authorities and meet the standards of the American Camping Association. The natural area around the site should be large enough to handle the number of students utilizing the facility and should contain sufficient variety to offer a range of study activities broad enough to accomplish the desired educational goals and objectives.

STAFFING

The length of the outdoor school operation and the budget usually determine the number and type of staff that can be realistically employed. Short term programs usually depend upon the resources of the classroom teachers and volunteers from the community. The seasonal and year-round operations will most likely have an on-site director plus a staff of field teachers. In addition to the classroom teachers, other personnel include a nurse, cook, maintenance workers, and cabin counselors.

Variations do occur in that some programs make arrangements with nearby colleges or universities for use of student teachers or interns as field teachers. Some programs allow high school students, parents, or community volunteers to serve as cabin counselors, whereas other centers employ a permanent staff to perform this role. In order to ensure proper supervision and quality instruction, the living group ratio should be approximately one leader to 8-10 children, while the field study group should not exceed 15 people per leader.

FINANCING

The fiscal support base and sources of funding also vary. A school unit might utilize any one, or combination of the following means:

a) Self-Support: The children and/or parents pay all the expenses. A portion of the funds might be raised through class projects such as cake sales, car washes, recycling projects, etc.
b) Parent-School Support: The parents contribute an amount equal to the cost of room, board, and accident insurance. The school unit budgets an amount that will cover instructional expense such as staff salaries, staff room and board, special materials and equipment, and transportation.
c) School Support: Funding from special government projects, PTAs, or other community groups enable some school units to pay the total expenses of the program.

TRANSPORTATION

Public school buses or rented common carriers are preferred over the use of private vehicles for transporting pupils. Local school codes and state laws should be checked closely for particular requirements.

MEDICAL SERVICES

If possible, a registered nurse should be in residence at the outdoor center, with the services of a medical doctor and clinic nearby. It is wise to have each child receive a medical clearance from either the family physician or the school nurse before participating. The teaching personnel should have general first aid knowledge and skill.

SPECIAL RESIDENT PROJECTS

Some interesting variations of the resident outdoor school have been tried in an attempt to meet the concerns of youth with special needs: potential drop-outs; physically handicapped; low-motivation. In both of the following examples, the basic values and purposes of a "resident" program are applied.

DECENTRALIZED CAMPING

This summer program took youth from "low-income families" to a wilderness area for a primitive, decentralized camping program. A rustic setting was chosen by design in order to expose the students to a "new world" and to serve as a catalyst in fostering social interaction. The counselors were regular teachers, from the school, and student teachers who had participated in a special leadership training workshop. The co-ed group was divided into three living units of twelve children and three adults. Two of the adults were teachers who would stay with the living group for the entire ten-day session. The third adult was the site leader who remained at the campsite while the groups rotated through on a round-robin basis every third day. In this manner, each unit participated in outdoor learning experiences at three different sites under the supervision of their teacher-counselors and site-specialist.

The purpose of the project was to accomplish the following goals by providing a resident outdoor experience that contained deep personal involvement with the basic essentials of the group-living process:

a) to broaden the experimental and educational horizons of youth
b) to promote healthier human relations
c) to increase the motivation to want to learn
d) to improve communication skills
e) to develop appreciation of the beauty and order of our natural environment
f) to enable teachers to work more effectively with culturally disadvantaged youth.

Various activities were selected as experiences that might enable the children to "open up" their sensory apparatus and "tune in" on the many unknowns of the outdoor world. An attempt was made to capitalize upon the curiosity "of the moment" and "on the spot" interests. The leaders used the sensory and problem-solving approach as much as possible.

Major learning activities at each site were:

1. Tepee Site: Located in a mountain meadow near a stream.
   Gold panning . . . nature hikes . . . visit to gold mine . . . fishing . . . archery . . . geology . . . star study . . . use of telescope.
2. Volcano Lake: Pupils had to pack in their supplies to reach this site on the shore of a beautiful crater-type lake.
   Campcraft . . . rock study . . . map and compass cross-country hike . . . bird study . . . fishing and rafting . . . swimming . . . exploration of old gold mine road and remains of an old mine and stamp mill.
3. Dugan's Pond: A shallow lake with considerable animal life nearby.

Hike to Sierra Buttes (the highest mountain in the area, 8587′) . . . visit to U.S. Forest Service fire lookout tower . . . swimming . . . plant study . . . animal homes . . . storytelling . . . star study . . . horseback riding.

MOBILE OR TRAVEL CAMPING

Another alternative to the centralized resident program is to conduct a mobile or traveling outdoor school. The overnight stays may be at campsites (county, state, or national parks) or indoor accommodations (schools, YMCAs, missions).

One junior high school planned a 1000-mile trip that took the students through a portion of their state rich in history, geology, and natural beauty. The travel unit consisted of twenty youngsters and five leaders in two minibuses and a pick-up truck. The following itinerary, although localized to California, can be duplicated in other states with appropriate changes:

1st Day: Starting point to Sutter's Fort (Sacramento) and Marshall Gold Discovery Site State Park (Coloma)

2nd Day: Coloma to Sierra Buttes Recreation Area (Tahoe National Forest) following the "Golden Chain," State Highway 49. Stop and explore gold mining towns of Auburn, Grass Valley, Downieville. Swim in the Yuba River.

3rd to Sierra Buttes Recreation Area: visit Plumas-Eureka State Park
5th Day: (museum on early California history, stamp mill plus mining equipment and relics); Frazer Falls, Mill's Peak Fire Lookout; Lincoln Valley. Swimming at Sand Pond; boating and fishing at the Sardine Lakes.

6th Day: Sierra Buttes Recreation Area to Fallen Leaf Lake with stops at Donner Party campsite and Donner State Park. Journey along western shore of Lake Tahoe.

7th to Fallen Leaf Lake Campground: visit Lake Tahoe, Rainbow Trail, U.S.
9th Day: Forest Service Stream Profile Chamber, Washoe Trail, Geology Trail, Angola Lookout. Attend evening campfires at Lake Tahoe amphitheater. Boatrides on Lake Tahoe and Echo Lakes. Horseback riding at stables. Swimming in lakes.

10th Day: Return home via Echo Pass.

It can be readily seen that the above program offers countless opportunities for learning experiences related to history, geography, conservation, geology, ecology, natural history, mathematics, and recreation.

An urban high school sponsored an "American Southwestern Study Tour" during the spring vacation period. This group, consisting of thirty-two students and eight leaders, journeyed 2,500 miles in a bus through the Southwest. The areas visited included: The Mojave Desert, Death Valley, Lake Mead, Zion

National Park, Lake Powell, Glen Canyon National Park. The collective goals included an intensive investigation of the geology, biology, and ecology of the region. The natural history of the Southwest was explored by bus, boat, and on foot.

IMPLEMENTATION

The resident outdoor school is an extension of the classroom into the out-of-doors in order to achieve certain curriculum objectives in an effective and efficient manner. How are these objectives implemented? What will take place at the outdoor school?

A few firsthand learning experiences that relate to study topics designated by students in the first model are:

    I. Flowers and Seeds
       A. Dissecting a flower in order to identify its parts.
       B. Keying out flowers in the field.
   II. Water Plants and Animals
       A. Making plaster casts of tracks near a river.
       B. Comparing the physical structure of water plants to land plants.

Moving in for a week of learning
and living in the out-of-doors.

A fossil reveals life through the ages.

III. Measurement
   A. Using a plane table to make map of the site.
   B. Estimating the width of a river by three different methods.
IV. Trees
   A. Using an increment borer to find the age of a tree.
   B. Comparing trees growing near the river to those growing on a hill.
 V. Rocks and Fossils
   A. Using a hardness set in comparing specimens found in the field.
   B. Determining the specific gravity of each rock found.
VI. Insects and Small Plants
   A. Observation to determine which plants certain insects prefer.
   B. Testing and comparing soil samples from areas where plants are plentiful with areas where vegetation is sparse.

The above activities concern *General Educational Goal I*—To complement the subject matter areas and the objectives of education through direct experience. Other goals are implemented as the various aspects of the educational program planned in the classroom are executed. The degree to which these goals are achieved is dependent, for the most part, on how the plans are executed rather than on what has been planned. Creation of an atmosphere that crackles with enthusiasm and excitement and wonder is the first duty of the outdoor school staff. Although the following goals are formally stated, they are usually "caught" rather than "taught" in the formal sense of the word. They are "lessons" learned from people who are deeply and closely involved in a common endeavor.

Goal II—To develop a realization of self. Progress toward this goal is going on all the time. The resident situation presents an opportunity for the individual to venture on his own in a community without competition from parents or from standards of the adult world. Although the outdoor school cannot guarantee a gift of self or self-discovery of individuality and worth, it certainly can create a climate within which self-discovery might progress.

In spite of careful planning in the classroom, this area is "played by ear" as the teachable moments occur in the 24-hour classroom.

Goal III—To develop understanding and appreciation of the out-of-doors. The

Total learning involves direct experience.

entire program is geared in this direction. Understanding is gained from daily study hikes and appreciation is developed from within as a result of the many firsthand contacts with nature. One advantage of the teaching-learning situation in the outdoors is nearness to the thing being studied. As many senses are brought into play, the learner becomes more involved. This involvement tends to develop interest that is genuinely intrinsic.

Goal IV—To develop a sense of physical well-being. Although a discussion of personal hygiene may take place during the planning stages, it is direct application of principles in daily living that causes them to become habits. Teachings started in the home are reinforced when the children eat nutritious meals that they themselves have planned, brush their teeth twice a day, and wash regularly.

Realization that the body is an instrument of expression may be related to hiking, climbing, dancing, and general recreational activity.

Goal V—To develop desirable human relationships and sound social attitudes, values, and concepts. The total program, including classroom planning and

Arithmetic is not forgotten during a week of resident outdoor education.

Pupils add their contribution to the outdoor school site
by working on a service project.

evaluating experiences before and after the resident period at the outdoor school, is designed and executed with this goal in mind. The numerous interactions between a small group for 24 hours a day over several days permit the resident school to become a human relations laboratory. The children have an opportunity to carry out their original plans concerning clean-up and housekeeping duties, setting tables and washing dishes, running the store and bank, and living together congenially in a miniature community. In a setting such as this, it is possible for the individual to develop deeper insights into the reasons for accepting and sharing responsibility, getting along with others, and understanding of an appreciation for group living and planning.

CLASSROOM FOLLOW-UP

The resident outdoor school experience extends back to the regular classroom before it can be said that the project is completed. Often, reference is made to the "pre-," "at," and "post" portion of the outdoor school program with most of the emphasis and effort placed upon the "at" period. In the well-integrated program, such a division is convenient for descriptive purposes only. Leaving out or de-emphasizing any one of the periods of the program decreases the potential value of the total experience. The portion of the experience executed at the resident outdoor school is complementary to the planning, organizing, follow-up, and evaluation that take place. It is for this reason that the classroom teacher should coordinate the entire sequence; he is the only person who shares all stages of the program with the children. He is the person best acquainted with the backgrounds of individual pupils and most familiar with the total curriculum for the year. Viewed in this manner, the outdoor school and its permanent field staff, specialists, and equipment are resources available to the teacher in order for him to achieve his goals and objectives in the most effective and efficient manner possible.

Returning to the classroom, it is wise for the class to review the original planning and the activities carried out at the resident school before deciding

Arithmetic and art are combined in a follow-up project.

what comes next. In our mythical class, the teacher's notes revealed the following plans discussed by the pupils:

    I. Classify and identify all collections and specimens brought back with us.
   II. Learn more about these specimens from our books and library.
  III. Share our materials and learnings with others—our parents and other classes—by preparing an exhibit and telling them about our displays.
  IV. Return equipment to owners.
   V. Write "thank you" letters.
  VI. Report to newspapers.
 VII. Exhibit sketches and paintings.
VIII. Evaluate what we did:
    A. Check original list, "Why are we going?"
    B. Ask ourselves questions:
      a. Was it worthwhile to go?
      2. What did we learn at the outdoor school?
      3. What did we enjoy most? Why?
      4. List new interests.
      5. If we go again, what could we do better?"

May 20 (9:30-10:30 A.M.) Closing our outdoor school account.

Store Inventory on May 12

Item	Quantity	Price	Cost
Stamps	50	8¢ each	
Milky Ways	78	3 for 25¢	
Nestles Crunches	78	5¢ each	
Peppermint Sticks	60	1 pkg. 29¢	
Pencils	10	3 pkgs. 29¢	
Envelopes	48	3 pkgs. @ 10¢	
Memo Pads	4	5¢ each	
		Total	

Store Inventory on May 16

Item	Quantity	No. Sold	Unit Price	Amount
Stamps	28		@ .08	
Milky Ways	30		@ .10	
Nestles Crunches	0		@ .05	
Peppermint Sticks	0		@ .01	
Pencils	6		@ .03	
Envelopes	23		@ .01	
Memo Pads	0		@ .05	
			Total	

How do we determine whether the store had a profit or loss?

How much?

What amount of money is still in unsold items?

May 21 (10:30–11:15 A.M.) Planning for our parents' night to be held on June 2 at 7:30 P.M.

1. Terrariums—tell about what's inside.
2. Display sketches and photographs.
3. Leaf prints—labels will tell about the different trees.
4. Rock display—samples of different types and kinds found.
5. Plaster casts—label and tell about animals seen.
6. Study hike reports—two people from each group.
7. Insects—mount and identify.
8. Square dance—demonstrate with student caller.
9. Display individual logs.

(1:15–2:00 P.M.)

Partial list of vocabulary learned at the outdoor school:

algae	photosynthesis
tributary	conifers
angiosperm	fungus
dicot	larva
monocot	erosion
parasite	salamander
saprophyte	fossil
chlorophyll	amphibians
lichen	lobed
pigments	dissect

May 22 (9:00–10:00 A.M.) Unfinished business. Some topics the class wanted to check on were:

I. Various growing things seen:
   A. bacteria   D. fungus
   B. mold   E. moss
   C. lichen   F. fern
II. Things all plants need in order to live.
III. Different ways a new plant can grow from an old one.

Other topics were approached in similar fashion. The major factor was that the "things" studied or questioned grew out of firsthand experiences at the resident outdoor school. Student teachers and parents, as well as pupils, were asked to fill out evaluation forms. (see samples on pp. 131–135).

SUMMARY

Variety and diversity are the words that best describe the types of resident outdoor school programs that are being conducted in North America today. Many factors determine the exact pattern of organization for a particular program: personnel, site, finances, philosophy, and local school laws.

The key factor, in spite of the wide range of practices, is that the development of a resident outdoor school can add a new dimension to the total educational program of a child. The classroom teacher, by becoming directly involved, may relate to his pupils in an entirely new manner which will enable him to vitalize teaching and learning both inside and outside the classroom.

SELECTED READINGS

Donaldson, George W. "A Camp Director Looks at His Program." *Journal of Educational Sociology* 25:529-32, May, 1950.

_____. *School Camping*. New York: Association Press, 1952.

*Donaldson, George W., and Hope A. Lambert. "School Camp—Outdoor Laboratory for Enriched Learning Experiences." *Camping Magazine* 28:17-21, May, 1956.

Green, Charlotte H. "Greensboro's Camp School." *Nature Magazine* 49:371-74, August, 1956.

Hubbard, Ruth A. "Three Teachers Start a School Camp." *National Elementary School Principal* 28:36-38, February, 1949.

Manley, Helen, and C. Drury. *Education Through School Camping*. St. Louis: C. V. Mosby Co., 1952.

Otto, C. Lucille. "Our Winter Outdoor School." *Journal of Health, Physical Education, Recreation* 28:3-9, December, 1957.

*Pike, Kenneth V. "The Long Beach Public School Camp." *National Elementary School Principal* 28:24-28, February, 1949.

Willard, Lotene. "Year Round Public School Camping." *National Education Association Journal* 38:576-77, November, 1949.

SELECTED MANUALS AND HANDBOOKS
FOR
RESIDENT OUTDOOR PROGRAMS

Bellevue Public Schools, "Student Leader Guide to the Bellevue Outdoor School." Bellevue Public Schools, Bellevue, Washington (revised, 1971)

*These articles may be found in *Outdoor Education: A Book of Readings* by Hammerman and Hammerman (Minneapolis: Burgess Publishing Company, 1973).

Chicago Public Schools, "Outdoor Education and Camping Program." ESEA Title I, 1965

Cleveland Heights Public Schools, "Laying the Trail—A Handbook for Teachers at the Cleveland Heights Outdoor School." Cleveland Heights, Ohio, 1963

Department of Public Instruction, "Guide to School Camping for Wisconsin." 1956

Gilfallen, Warren, and Robert Burgess, "The Teacher's Handbook for the Outdoor School." Multnomah County, Portland, Oregon, 1968

Marin County Superintendent of Schools, "A Curriculum Guide for Marin County's Resident Outdoor School." Marin County, California, 1966

Niagara South Board of Education, "St. Johns Outdoor Studies Centre Programme." St. Johns West, Fonthill, Ontario, Canada

Roller, Elizabeth, "Outdoor Education Manual for the Nature-Resource Center." Metropolitan Nashville-Davidson County Schools, Nashville, Tennessee

Snell, Blanche E., "Albion Hills Conservation School." The Metropolitan Toronto and Region Conservation Authority, Woodbridge, Ontario, 1963

Toronto Board of Education, "Island Natural Science School." Toronto Board of Education, 1970

Wade, Douglas E. (Editor), "Outdoor Education Handbook." Department of Outdoor Teacher Education, Northern Illinois University Taft Campus, Oregon, Illinois (revised, 1969)

Chapter VI
Implications for
Teacher Education
in Outdoor Education

There is continuing evidence that outdoor education in its varied forms is well entrenched in many public school systems, and continues to expand at an ever-increasing rate. Extending the classroom into the natural environment out-of-doors provides the climate for implementing educational objectives. This is accomplished by means of a direct experience, multi-sensory approach to learning which is far more meaningful than vicarious experience alone. Furthermore, firsthand learning tends to reinforce and enrich the multiplicity of knowledge learned at second hand in the somewhat artificial context of the classroom.

What are the implications for teacher education? First, several basic needs should be identified. We should first recognize the psychological soundness of the outdoor education approach to teaching and learning based on what we know to be effective instructional techniques for facilitating efficient and lasting learning. Second, we should recognize the need for classroom teachers with the knowledge and skills that will enable them to teach as effectively outside the school as they do inside the classroom.

If we accept the logic of these two basic needs, this points up a third need—namely, the need for preparing teachers with the competencies and skills that will enable them to carry on effective teaching in a variety of instructional environments beyond the schoolroom. This need for professional preparation of teachers in outdoor education should take place at both the pre-service and the in-service level.

PRE-SERVICE OUTDOOR TEACHER EDUCATION

Professional preparation in outdoor education at the pre-service or undergraduate level should have three primary areas of emphasis.

1. Outdoor education as a means to more effective and efficient learning.
2. Relating the school curriculum to the out-of-doors.
3. The out-of-doors as a practical laboratory for living and learning.

OUTDOOR EDUCATION IS A MEANS TO EFFICIENT AND EFFECTIVE LEARNING

We know that a great quantity of subject matter is presented at second and third hand in the classroom. Education in the out-of-doors is a method of providing future teachers with insight and understanding into the nature of the

Teachers, too, need time to relate abstract knowledge to the world of reality.

learning process. How is this accomplished? By going to the natural environment and searching for the answers to such questions as:

1. How do we learn?
2. What is the difference between sensing and perceiving?
3. How does multi-sensory perception enhance learning?
4. How do children form concepts?
5. What steps are involved in problem solving, and how can these steps be applied to investigating what one does not know?
6. How can one develop a sensory awareness of his surroundings?
7. What skills are involved in recording one's observations of the unfamiliar or the unknown?
8. What qualities characterize a "teachable moment" and how may the teacher capitalize on these moments when they occur in the natural environment?
9. What teaching procedures are particularly suitable or appropriate for outdoor instruction, or does the natural environment require new and different teaching techniques?

Exploring questions like these constitute the basis for an introduction to teaching out-of-doors. Searching for answers to the above questions exposes the pre-service teacher to a variety of outdoor learning experiences.

Sensation and perception. Students are guided through a series of experiences that enable them to "open up" all of their sensory apparatus and "tune in" on the many unknowns in the outdoor environment. Hearing a noise or sound and not knowing what it is, is an example of simple sensation. The initial sensation is without meaning. If the learner traces the sound to its source, discovers that a bird is calling, and through close observation and by checking data in a bird guide arrives at the conclusion that the sound he hears is the song of a cardinal—the sensation assumes meaning for the learner. When external stimuli take on meaning or value in this fashion, these "unknown" sensations become "known," therefore perceived.

Much of what we learn is acquired perceptually. It is highly important that the professional educator, if he is to be successful in teaching, understand the significance of this fundamental aspect of the learning process. It is almost axiomatic in education that subject matter perceived by more than one sense will make a far greater impact on the learner.

Generally speaking, that which is learned through multi-sensory perception is learned more readily and is retained longer than that which is learned involving one sense only. Essential knowledge about plants, for example, will be acquired more readily and retained far longer if the senses of sight, touch, taste, and smell have been involved, as opposed to simply reading factual information about the plants.

Problem-solving. The essence of learning in real life is through problem-solving, a process uncommon in many classrooms. This process, briefly stated, finds the learner becoming involved in purposeful planning. The learner rather than the teacher seeks to establish or identify a goal that is worthy to him. The learner then devises a plan for achieving the goal. The learner or learners either individually or collectively then try the plan. If on the first trial it does not lead to a successful solution of the problem, a revision or modification of the plan is devised and successive tries are made until the desired goal is reached.

This is the way we ordinarily operate outside of the classroom. It is the way most of us learn when we are sufficiently curious about something to want to investigate it on our own.

The outdoor setting free of the usual classroom stereotypes is especially conducive to problem-solving. Teachers-in-training should understand the steps involved in problem-solving. Furthermore, they need to become adept at recognizing opportunities for problem-solving and ought to experience problem-solving themselves before attempting it with youngsters in the field. Examples of outdoor problem-solving are presented in Chapter III.

A frequently neglected aspect of the scientific approach is a consideration of

Let's "find out" is the byword in outdoor study.

the need for and the techniques of close and accurate observation. The natural environment is an ideal laboratory in which to develop and refine the skills of observing closely and then recording accurately what one has perceived. If today's teachers are charged with the responsibility of educating tomorrow's scientists, the teachers themselves must be adept in ways of observing the strange and the unfamiliar in order to better comprehend what one sees. They must learn to sift through their observations and pick out distinguishing characteristics as well as to express their perception in such a way that the evidence gathered is understandable and communicates meaning.

Outdoor teaching techniques. Traditional classroom teaching techniques do not ordinarily involve methods such as developing a clue chart or employing an exploratory approach to learning. (These methods are discussed in detail in Chapter III.) Pre-service teachers should be provided an opportunity to acquire the competencies that will enable them to teach effectively outside as well as inside the school. We find, of course, that many classroom teaching techniques are every bit as appropriate for outdoor instruction as for indoor teaching. The

Pre-service teachers discover that all knowledge is not found in a book.

Socratic method of questioning and problem solving are two methods that lend themselves quite suitably to outdoor teaching as well as to in-school instruction.

The teacher bold enough to venture beyond the classroom must be able to capitalize upon pupil curiosity and interest as it develops on the spot. This requires imagination along with the ability to interrupt "the lesson" for a few moments to pursue on-the-spot investigation of a newfound discovery. Frequently the teacher outdoors finds that he must be able to play part of the lesson by ear in order to capitalize on the countless *unplanned* teaching opportunities that invariably crop up while exploring in the field. Pre-service teachers-in-training should recognize that all knowledge is not to be found "in-the-book." The flexible and imaginative approach will, more often than not, reap tremendous dividends in terms of the genuine concerns and interests of the learner.

Outdoor teacher education should be integrated into the professional program to investigate the various sources of knowledge. The out-of-doors literally becomes a laboratory for investigating appropriate aspects of educational psychology dealing with how man develops concepts, gains insight, acquires knowledge, develops appreciations, and changes attitudes.

Outdoor teacher education is a vehicle for providing teachers with additional insight into (1) the natural environment, (2) the learning process, and (3) the child as a learner. A few of these insights are listed below:

Insights into the natural environment:

1. The out-of-doors is part of a grand design.
2. Plants and animals are part of a complex system of survival checks and balances.
3. Many plants and animals adapt uniquely to a particular environmental setting.
4. Birth, growth, death, and decay are constants in the natural environment ... and death and decay are essential to birth and growth.
5. Plants and animals often reveal a natural cyclical rhythm in their growth.
6. Climatic conditions influence the natural environment.

7. Nature's web is easily broken by changing conditions.
8. Adaptation is essential for survival.

Insights into the learning process:

1. We learn by being told.
2. We learn by imitation.
3. We learn through the use of our senses: seeing, hearing, touching, tasting, and smelling.
4. We learn by observing.
5. We learn by asking questions.
6. We learn by identifying and relating what we already know to what we don't know.
7. We learn by researching for what we don't know.
8. We learn through the use of equipment such as books, records, binoculars, compasses, etc.
9. We learn by trial and error.

A future teacher ponders the interrelatedness of knowledge beyond
the four walls of the schoolroom.

10. We learn by experimentation.
11. We learn by comparing.
12. We learn by performing.
13. We learn by experience.

Insights into understanding the child as a learner:

1. Children may have different concepts of the same thing.
2. Children like to have fun.
3. Children are innately curious.
4. Children seek adventure.
5. Children want to participate in new experiences.

Every teacher needs to understand the child as a learner in the learning process. Learning can be facilitated, enriched, and reinforced through knowledge of the natural environment and recognition of the possibilities for relating firsthand observation and direct experience to the school curriculum.

RELATING THE SCHOOL CURRICULUM TO THE OUT-OF-DOORS

Professional educators caught in the lockstep of tradition may experience difficulty in recognizing educational possibilities for taking youngsters out of the classroom in order to learn. A main objective of teacher education, therefore, should be to include experiences in the professional preparation of teachers that will provide increased awareness and understanding of the relationship of outdoor learning experience to the school curriculum. To meet this objective students should be instructed in a variety of outdoor learning activities and teaching techniques in each basic area of the curriculum that would enrich and complement classroom instruction. Incorporated into this phase of study would be preparation of lesson plans and presentation of outdoor lessons.

Examples of subject matter which can be reinforced, vitalized, and made more meaningful through firsthand learning in the out-of-doors appear below:

Language Arts

While investigating various ways of utilizing the out-of-doors in relation to language arts, students may carry out activities such as:

1. Finding a nature specimen in the woods or field and checking it out in a resource book.
2. Listening to various bird songs and recording the sound in schematic diagrams.
3. Reading or telling stories around the campfire.
4. Reading about the local history of the area after becoming acquainted firsthand with places, people, and events of historical interest.
5. Writing about an outdoor experience.

Mathematics

Students investigate ways of using mathematics in the out-of-doors and attempt to relate fundamental arithmetic processes to the natural environment.

 1. Measure the height of a tree or the width of a river or valley by any one of several indirect methods of measurement (see Chapter III).
 2. Determine the slope of a hill.
 3. Learn to use a compass.
 4. Construct a map to scale.
 5. Pace off an acre.
 6. Measure the circumference and diameter of trees.
 7. Figure the rate of flow of a river or creek.
 8. Compute the distance traveled on a hike.
 9. Estimate wind velocity.
10. Measure precipitation (rain or snow).

Science

Students can explore, discover, collect specimens, and record information pertinent to:

 1. Botany, zoology, and geology.
 2. Observing and recording weather data.
 3. Locating and identifying constellations in the night sky.
 4. Identifying surface features of the moon through a spotting scope.
 5. Collecting and testing soil samples.

The list of science activities appropriate to outdoor study is virtually inexhaustable. For this reason only a small sampling of activities is presented here. Additional areas of study for which pre-service teachers require professional preparation are mentioned in Chapter III.

Social Studies

 1. Observe the physical geography of an area and analyze how man has adapted to it.
 2. Construct maps of the area.
 3. Study history in the field: visit a cemetery, explore Indian mounds and cliff dweller ruins.

Music and Art

Students may attempt to stimulate and release inherent creative impulses through an increased awareness to beauty which exists, in varied forms, in the natural world.

 1. Use weeds, seeds, and grasses to create a nature picture.
 2. Sketch or paint using natural pigments only.

3. Find a natural deposit of clay, refine it, work it.
4. Make a musical instrument from indigenous materials.
5. Compose a song from sounds in nature.

Physical Education and Recreation

Pupils should receive instruction in physical education activities and leisure time skills that have carryover value to and through the years of adulthood. These would include such skills as: fishing, swimming, canoeing, archery, hunting, and skiing.

PRACTICUM IN OUTDOOR TEACHER EDUCATION

Every professional teacher education program should include a practicum in outdoor teacher education. Education majors, preferably at the senior level, would spend one school week (five days) in residence with pupils at an outdoor school facility. The week of living with and instructing youngsters in the outdoor school setting would be a valuable supplement to the regular student teaching experience.

Student teachers acquire instructional resourcefulness.

The outdoor teacher education practicum may have a slightly different focus depending upon when it is scheduled in the professional education sequence. For example, if the outdoor education practicum is scheduled prior to student teaching it may be utilized as an introduction to student teaching. This provides the student teacher an opportunity to experiment with teaching method, and to test through practical application some of the educational theories that he has been exposed to in his more formal classwork.

On the other hand, the outdoor teacher education practicum may be scheduled following the regular student teaching experience. If this is the case, in addition to experimenting with method and testing theory and procedure, the emphasis is upon reinforcing teaching skills which the student has developed during his student teaching.

Due to the number of student teachers and youngsters in residence it may be difficult for each student teacher to teach the entire class of pupils at any one time. To solve this problem, a teaching team plan may be implemented. A class of thirty children, for example, is divided into five small groups of six each. The classroom teacher may group youngsters according to the results of a socio-metric device, or according to pupil interest. A teaching team of four or five

Teachers gain additional insight into pupil behavior
in the informal, total-living situation.

student teachers is assigned to work with each of the small self-contained groups of youngsters. The composition of the children's groups and the teaching teams remains constant throughout the resident outdoor school experience. Each small group has a designated meeting place for its planning sessions. These meeting places should be equipped with a planning board or portable chalkboard and a "portable library."

The student teachers in each teaching team are confronted with and have to work out satisfactory solutions to many of the same problems that face a school faculty. After developing initial plans with the youngsters the student teachers work out their own teaching assignments. They need to locate suitable instructional materials, and prepare their lessons.

It is best not to overwhelm the pupils with an overdose of adult supervision. A desirable pattern of operation is to have only two members of a teaching team with the pupils at any one time—one teaching, the other observing. The observing member of the team records such things as: children's reactions to certain learning situations, incidental learnings which may occur on the trip, questions posed by pupils, and child behavior in general. This information may then be shared with the regular classroom teacher so that he may follow through effectively in the classroom.

This arrangement frees at least two members of each teaching team either in the morning or the afternoon. Student teachers may utilize this time in a number of ways; some prepare their teaching assignments, others record their observations, while others meet in informal discussion with the classroom teacher or their own supervising professor to analyze the experiences which they and the children are having.

In addition to teaching youngsters in the outdoor classroom, student teachers also assume responsibility for supervising the dining hall where children set tables and serve as hosts and hostesses. Student teachers supervise "Big Housekeeping," the "Quiet Hour," evening recreation, and putting children to bed at the end of the day.

The teaching team arrangement provides an organizational framework that allows for a unique student teaching experience. (1) Student teachers are able to work with a small group of children rather intensively in a resident situation. (2) The student teacher assumes total responsibility for the pupils assigned to him during their stay at the outdoor school. (3) Student teachers have the opportunity to plan and evaluate daily with children. (4) Student teachers are able to handle and discuss problems of administration and organization at a professional level among themselves. (5) Within this organizational framework continuity can be developed from morning to afternoon activity period as well as from day to day. (6) The student teacher has the opportunity to promote and develop follow-up activities with pupils. (7) The teaching team structure affords an opportunity to operate within a highly flexible schedule.

This practicum in outdoor teacher education is a unique opportunity for the pre-service teacher to work with children in an informal total-living situation. Institutions of higher education are discovering that experiences of this type have a singular result, namely: teachers who develop a high degree of competency for teaching both inside and outside of the schoolroom.

EVALUATING OUTDOOR TEACHER EDUCATION

Evaluation is a continual process. During and immediately following the professional laboratory experience outdoors student teachers carry on some form of evaluation. This may take either written or verbal form, or a combination of both. There is no standard pattern for evaluating the outdoor teaching practicum. Student teachers should devise the approach and any written instruments that they wish to use in evaluating the experience. Two examples should suffice to illustrate the manner in which the problem of evaluation may be handled by teachers-in-training.

Class A decides that each student teacher will respond in writing to the following two questions: (1) In your opinion what is the greatest single contribution that this experience can make to a program of teacher education? (2) What things do you think you will do with your class next year which you might not have done without this experience?

These questions were actually answered by senior students following an outdoor student teaching experience. Representative responses were:

— I believe that the greatest single contribution is that this experience can broaden a teacher's scope of educational method—that all learning is not always best gotten from a book. Through the use of outdoor experiences many learning activities can be more thoroughly understood. It gives opportunity for practical application of skills in everyday living.

— I hadn't realized the many possibilities for teaching outside the classroom. Nature hikes seemed to be the extent of my use of the out-of-doors. After my week's experience I found that nearly every subject matter area can be taught in the out-of-doors.

— In my opinion, the greatest single contribution which a week such as we have just had can make to a program of teacher education is making the teacher aware of the out-of-doors and how she can use it in her classroom teaching. . . . Spending a week educating the teacher is only a small matter if the purpose of making her aware is achieved.

— Things I think I will do next year as a result of my week's experience are: to make terrariums, and to make a "natural materials" Christmas tree using weeds, leaves, and seeds for the decorations. I want to take my students outdoors to listen for sounds and to notice differences among trees.

— I plan to make more effective use of the materials which children bring into the classroom. . . . I believe that science is a means of interesting the disinterested child. There is always a stick, a stone, or an insect about which he is curious.

— In teaching next year I will constantly look for opportunitites to give my children as many outdoor experiences as possible. I will teach the things that can be taught out-of-doors best outside the classroom. I feel that if children are given these direct experiences they will retain what they learn for a longer period of time. In using these experiences with children I will try to see that they understand what they are learning. In other words, they will have a chance to evaluate their learning experiences.

— Heretofore I have used the out-of-doors for science, but have limited it to that phase of study. I will incorporate the first-hand experiences into other phases of education when I think they will deepen understanding. When children ask questions I will encourage them to seek the answer for themselves. I plan to take a more active interest in natural specimens brought to class by the children.

Class B decided to evaluate their week of outdoor teacher education by having each student teacher respond to the following questionnaire which they titled, "Evaluation of Professional Growth of Student Teachers."

(1) What insights have I gained in group relations?
The insights I have gained from working with this sixth grade group are as follows: (a) The adult approval is beginning to lose some importance to the preadolescent, and peer group approval is now of greater importance. (b) Gangs are especially strong—boys with boys, girls with girls. (c) The preadolescent age group can work cooperatively in groups or teams.

(2) What insights have I gained into better understanding of individual behavior?
We must see the whole picture before we can understand behavior in an individual child. For example, individual behavior results, very often, from relations with others. Children at this age also move back and forth between the childish behavior they are outgrowing and the more mature behavior they are growing into.

(3) What progress have I made in my teaching techniques?
I made a great deal of use out of the technique of asking in order to stimulate thought. I also learned a very important fact. A teacher doesn't need to know all the answers. Often very good teaching is the result of teacher and pupils working together to discover the answer. I also gained extra practice in leading songs, which was extremely helpful because it gave me more confidence along this line.

(4) What progress have I made in my ability to help students use time wisely and creatively?
After checking the list of personal interests I tried to steer the children's leisure time activities along these lines. . . . After a hike I always tried to bring the group back in time so they could spend some time looking things up in the library.

(5) How have I improved my ability to organize pupil activities (planning, execution, evaluation)?
I feel that I have improved my ability to organize student activities by using a mental lesson plan. . . . This has helped me to see my objectives more clearly. Evaluation many times can be conducted very informally as shown by discussion on the trail and around the dinner table.

(6) In what situations have I been able to guide students in carrying out routines effectively?
. . . in those situations that were planned by the children and where I acted only as another member of the group giving suggestions when necessary.

(7) By the use of what specific devices have I been able to stimulate genuine student interest in the planned activities?
I think the use of concrete materials such as rocks, compasses, rock hammers, hand lenses and all the out-of-doors is about the best stimulation anyone needs. . . . by being enthusiastic myself—it seems to be contagious.

(8) Under what conditions have I been able to maintain group control?
In the dining room, in a small group meeting, on the trail and in the bunkhouse during rest hour. Let the children know you understand their difficulties and are interested in helping them.

Statements such as this reveal that undergraduate, pre-service teachers attach considerable significance to practical experience in outdoor education. The day is long past when a teacher can rest secure in his ability to confine knowledge solely to the classroom. There are just too many excellent instructional opportunities to limit learning to the school facility alone. In order for the modern teacher to take advantage of the wide variety of community resources and natural environment areas, every institution of higher education dedicated to the professional preparation of teachers should include outdoor teacher education in its curriculum.

IN-SERVICE TEACHER EDUCATION

The in-service teacher, usually experienced and secure with tenure, may tend to be somewhat slow to accept and put into practice a different way of doing things—especially if it means a radical readjustment of values or of procedure. For this reason he is sometimes a bit more difficult to reach when it comes to a new or slightly different approach to teaching and learning.

The idea of leaving the school building only for recess, physical education, or fire drill is well founded in tradition. It is often more difficult to shake the in-service teacher free from tradition than to influence the pre-service teacher who is in the midst of receiving his professional education.

What avenues, then, are available for bringing the outdoor education viewpoint, its philosophy, values, and procedures to the attention of the in-service educator? There are several tried and tested approaches. Outdoor education can be presented to in-service teachers through:

1. District or county teacher institutes during the school year.
2. A series of in-service workshops held in the field demonstrating various outdoor teaching procedures.
3. Weekend conferences or workshops at nearby teacher education institutions.

In-service teachers develop broad social studies concepts by
acquiring American Indian handicraft skills.

4. Films that depict outstanding program developments in outdoor education
   (see list at end of this chapter).
5. P.T.A. programs.
6. Calling on outdoor education authorities to provide consultant service to
   local school districts.
7. Summer school opportunities:
   a. Workshops and courses offered by colleges and universities.
   b. National Audubon Society programs and camps.
   c. National Science Foundation institutes.

In order for outdoor education to make its greatest contribution to American
public education it must be philosophically embraced, experimented with, and
put to the test by all teachers—the tenured and experienced teacher as well as
the fledgling instructor. Outdoor education provides the type of vital instructional resource and teaching medium that no school system can afford to be
without.

SELECTED READINGS

Bullington, Robert A. "When Teachers Go to Camp." *American Biology Teacher* 17:99-101, March, 1955.

*Conrad, Lawrence H. "The Teacher Out-of-Doors." *Bulletin of the National Association of Secondary School Principals* 31:36-41, May, 1947.

Cooper, Herman. "Teacher Education for the Out-of-Doors." *Bulletin of the National Association of Secondary School Principals* 31:53-59, May, 1947.

Hammerman, Donald R. *"Teacher Education Moves Outdoors."* Illinois Education *Journal* 43:350-51, May, 1957.

_____. "A Shot in the Arm for Teacher Education." *Journal of Health, Physical Education, Recreation* 29:21, November, 1958.

*_____. "First Hand Experiences for First Rate Teachers." *Journal of Teacher Education* 11:408-11, September, 1960.

Jaffe, Dorothea K. "Preparing Teachers to Teach Outdoors." *Nation's Schools* 55:47-50, June, 1955.

Klotz, J. W. "Outdoor Education at Concordia Teachers College." *American Biology Teacher* 17:266-69, December, 1955.

*Ozmon, Howard A., Jr. "College Experiment in the Out-of-Doors New Jersey School of Conservation, Stokes State Forest." *Journal of Health, Physical Education, Recreation* 33:30, April, 1962.

Vinal, William G. "Some Non-Traditional Practices in Training for Outdoor Leadership." *School Science and Math.* 53:521-35, October, 1953.

SELECTED FILMS ON OUTDOOR EDUCATION

AN APPROACH TO SCHOOL SITE DEVELOPMENT, University of Michigan, Ann Arbor, Michigan 48104

*These articles may be found in *Outdoor Education: A Book of Readings* by Hammerman and Hammerman (Minneapolis: Burgess Publishing Company, 1973).

CAMPING EDUCATION, 35 m. Illinois State Museum, Springfield, Illinois 62705

CHAPARREL CLASSROOM, 18 m. Media Distribution, Northern Illinois University, DeKalb, Illinois 60115 # 5050337

CLASSROOM IN THE CASCADES, 30 m. University of Washington, Seattle, Washington 98105

EDUCATION MOVES OUTDOORS, 18 m. Media Distribution, Northern Illinois University, DeKalb, Illinois 60115 #5050052

GREEN YEARS, Center For Urban Education, 105 Madison Ave., New York, N.Y. 10016

HOW WE LOOK AT THINGS, Kalamazoo Nature Center, 7000 N. Westnedge, Kalamazoo, Michigan 49001

I WENT TO THE WOODS, Antioch College Audio Visual Aids, Yellow Springs, Ohio 45387

JUST BEYOND THE CHALKBOARD, 25 m. Media Distribution, Northern Illinois University, DeKalb, Illinois 60115 #7050347

LEARNING IN AN OUTDOOR ENVIRONMENT, 21 m. Media Distribution, Northern Illinois University, DeKalb, Illinois 60115 #5050536

NATURE NEXT DOOR, Sierra Club, Mills Tower, San Francisco, California 94104

NATURE'S CLASSROOM, State Office Building, Madison, Wisconsin 53702

NEAR HOME, British Information Service, Radio City, New York, N.Y. 10019

OUTDOOR EDUCATION, Capital Film Service, Lansing, Michigan 48912

OUTDOOR EDUCATION IN COOK COUNTY, Forest Preserve District, 536 N.· Harlem Ave., River Forest, Illinois

SCHOOLTIME IN CAMP, 18 m. Media Distribution, Northern Illinois University, DeKalb, Illinois 60115 #5050101

TEACHER EDUCATION IN THE OUT-OF-DOORS, 20 m. Media Distribution, Northern Illinois University, DeKalb, Illinois 60115 #5050107

THE BIG ADVENTURE, 14 m. Conservation Education Section, Department of Natural Resources, State Office Building No. 1, Sacramento, California 95814

THE WINDOW, 20 m. National Audubon Society, Photo and Film Department, 1130 Fifth Ave. New York, N.Y. 10028

THIS IS SCICON, Tulare County Schools, AV Department, Court House, Visalia, California 93277

TO LIVE ON EARTH, 15 m. Media Distribution, Northern Illinois University, DeKalb, Illinois 60115 #5050552

WISDOM GROWS OUTDOORS, 22 m. Michigan Department of Conservation, Film Loan Service, Lansing, Michigan 48933

Chapter VII
Evaluation Procedures and Research Findings in Outdoor Education

Most educational ventures are considered incomplete until some type of evaluation procedure has been followed. Outdoor education experiences are no exception. Each activity should be scrutinized in order to determine the degree of success in accomplishing the desired learning goals and objectives. As education enters the era of accountability, teachers will be expected to substantiate various gains if the programs are to be continued.

EVALUATION PROCEDURES

The evaluation process begins when the general goals and specific objectives are identified. If they are clearly stated at the outset the task of selecting appropriate experiences and activities is simplified, and the framework for deciding the level of achievement is constructed. Many educators believe that the most effective way of stating specific learning objectives is behaviorally, i.e., a statement of what the learner will do in order to demonstrate achievement of the objective. The following examples contain the ingredients of sound performance objectives:

Given a number of different soil samples the learner will, with 80% accuracy, be able to describe and record in chart form the characteristics of each sample including: color, texture, pH, and ability to hold moisture.

Following a study plot exercise, the student will be able to construct, with 90% accuracy, a food chain diagram illustrating the animal-plant and animal-animal relationships within that particular plot.

Following a study hike in a forest community, each pupil should be able to express his feelings of awareness by one of the following means: in writing (haiku or cinquain); in a painting (water colors, ink, or oils); in a mosaic using native materials.

After a soil study lesson, the participant should be able to express (orally or in writing) his feelings about man's effect upon that particular soil environment.

Upon the completion of an orientation lesson in the use of a magnetic compass, 80% of the class members should be able to locate the hidden treasure at the end of a "destination unknown" hike.

After a field trip to a tree farm, lumber mill, or forest, each person should be able to estimate, with 90% accuracy, the number of board feet in selected trees by utilizing a Merritt Rule and Biltmore Stick.

It is a relatively simple task for the classroom teacher to determine whether or not a student has successfully met the requirements of these objectives. A closer inspection of the above examples will reveal that there are two for each of three domains for educational objectives—cognitive, affective, and psycho-motor skill. The final plan of evaluation should include not only items from all three major domains, but should also represent the various levels of depth. It must be kept in mind, however, that some behavioral phenomena still cannot be measured on a man-made instrument. Most fall in the affective domain. Some examples are: how does one measure the *thrill* of discovery, *appreciation* of a sunset, or a *sense of self-confidence* after conquering a difficult situation.

Recently, teachers have also been placing greater importance upon "learning how to learn"—the basic processes of learning. One such list includes:

Observation	Using Numbers
Inference	Measurement
Communication	Time/Space Relationships
Classification	Prediction

The American Association for the Advancement of Science has also prepared a list of learning processes that, in addition to the above, includes:

Formulating Hypotheses, Experimenting, and Interpreting.

These categories have become the central focus of some evaluation attempts whereby performance objectives are developed around one or more of the above processes. For example: After a study plot encounter, each student shall be able to:

a) Describe at least five ways in which man has affected that particular area. (Inference)

b) Predict what the plot will look like in five years, if it is allowed to exist in its present condition. (Prediction)

In order to obtain the data or evidence that will aid the evaluator in making a total assessment of an outdoor lesson or program, some of the following tools or instruments may prove helpful:

1. Sociogram: During evaluation discussions, the teacher might ask, "If we were to go to the resident outdoor school again, who would you want in your living group?" The follow-up sociogram resulting from these selections could then be compared with the initial diagram in order to detect changing patterns within the class.
   Note: It is obvious that the boys' acceptance of classmate #13 changed greatly. It would be interesting to know why this change took place. This type of insight might result if the teacher and staff utilized the next evaluation technique.
2. Anecdotal records: This form of recording direct observations of children in a variety of situations lends itself to detecting recurring patterns of behavior. Further analysis might reveal "what makes Johnny tick" and the kinds of circumstances that threaten him or provide support. The anecdotes should be a concise and objective account of what was said or done by the individual. Such data may provide valuable insight into the child's self-concept, value system, or attitudes.
3. Teacher-made tests: Essay and objective questions may be utilized by the teacher in an effort to find out how much information or conceptual understanding was gained by the student. Situation type questions can also be developed that will indicate the student's ability to perform various learning processes, i.e., predicting, classifying, etc.
4. Interviews: An extremely beneficial technique for evaluation is the personal interview with the individual. Although it may be time consuming, it may prove to be highly significant in obtaining insights. The teacher might use data from the sociogram or anecdotal records as the basis for some questions during the interview.
5. Daily logs: The logs kept by the children or the stories written following their return to the classroom might cast additional light on other benefits gained from a resident outdoor school program. Items mentioned in these writings might be useful in the individual interviews.
6. Creative projects: For those students who may not express themselves well verbally, much can be learned from their creative expressions such as sketches, paintings, sculptures, or musical compositions. Photographic stories by the children are an alternative art form that allows insights through the "eye of the beholder." Creative expressions frequently project those experiences that were most significant and meaningful to the creator.

7. Questionnaires: Although this information is subjective, questionnaire responses may be categorized to reveal significant gains and accomplishments of the program. Separate forms should be designed for use with pupils, parents, and teachers. (See samples on pp. 131-135.)

Sociogram of Boys' Choices for Cabin Mates

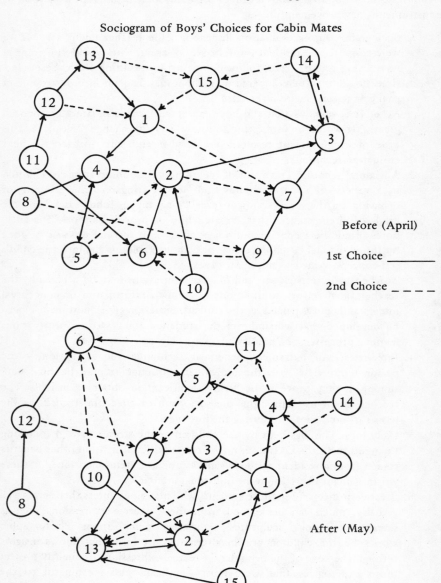

Before (April)

1st Choice _____

2nd Choice _ _ _ _

After (May)

SAMPLE PUPIL EVALUATION OF OUR
RESIDENT OUTDOOR SCHOOL PROGRAM

1. Was it worthwhile to go?
   Yes - _____   No - _____
2. What did you learn at the outdoor school?
   a. What a dicot and a monocot is
   b. How to measure height with a pencil or stick
   c. How to measure across a river
   d. How big an acre is
   e. New vocabulary words
   f. How to make a terrarium
   g. How to identify rocks and fossils
   h. How to be independent
   i. About stars and constellations
   j. The parts of a flower
   k. Difference between lizards and salamanders
   l. How old a fossil might be
   m. About the three stages of forest development
   n. How to identify birds
   o. How to tell poison ivy from other plants.
3. What did you enjoy most? Why?
   a. Cabin life because it was fun to sleep and eat with classmates
   b. Star-gazing because I learned new constellations
   c. Bird hike because I could see them in their natural habitats
   d. Fossil hunt because I like to see of what they are made
   e. Flower hike because we got to see them in the place where they live.
4. List any new interests you have or any changes you plan to make in the way
   you do things because of the outdoor school experience.
   a. Make my bed more often
   b. I am more interested in small animals
   c. I like to star-gaze
   d. I'd like to learn more about trees
   e. More interested in rocks and fossils
   f. I'm more interested in microscopic life
   g. I found out I was fat so now I am on a diet.
5. If we should go again, what could we do better?

SAMPLE PARENT EVALUATION OF A
RESIDENT OUTDOOR SCHOOL PROGRAM

1. Did this experience make a difference in your child?
   A. List any new interests your child has shown.

General nature (plants, animals, rocks, stars)
Care of house
Etiquette at table
Going to summer camp
Goes outside more instead of watching T.V.

B. List any changes in the way your child does things or in the way he carries on his daily routine.
Willing to help at home
More cheerful
Seems more mature
More independent—does things on his own
Willing to assume more responsibility
Thinks ahead in planning duties for next day
Neater in care of room and personal items
Willing to try different types of food.

C. List any evidence of changes in feelings of your child toward classmates or teacher.

Children develop a greater appreciation of the outdoor world.

Feels closer to group as a whole
More sensitive to approval of classmates than before
Greater regard for many other classmates
More appreciation of friendship
Greater realization of the "human side" of teachers and parents
Grownups have fun and comradeship as much as children.

2. Do you think the resident outdoor school was a worthwhile activity? Why?
   Yes - _____ No response - _____ I don't know - _____
   Cooperation—carrying out planned activities
   Eagerness and enthusiasm of the total project
   More aware of himself as a separate, independent individual
   Appreciation of the wonder of the "outside world"
   Understands how to get along with more than just a few friends
   Knowledge gained from study hikes
   Physical fitness from various activities
   Demands of responsibility and self-reliance
   Manners improved.

3. If we should plan another outdoor school program, what changes would you suggest?
   Try to get week to cost less
   Nice to have one full week—seven days.

SAMPLE TEACHER EVALUATION OF THE RESIDENT OUTDOOR SCHOOL

1. Did the resident outdoor school experience make a difference in your attitudes or philosophy?

   A. List some facts you learned or new ideas and thoughts that came to you as a result of this program.

      (1) I learned how to get along with the children and, in turn, I feel that they learned how to get along with each other.

      (2) Children are so eager to learn. The teacher does not have to know everything—the children do not expect her to. I think I learned as much subject matter as the children. Each time I went on a study hike I saw millions of things that I hadn't seen before.

      (3) One of the teachers made me realize, as he did the children, that everything in nature is related and necessary if life is to continue.

   B. List any new interests you have or any changes you plan to make in the way you do things that will influence your career as a teacher.

      (1) Some of the field trips I hope to be able to take my pupils on are:

         (a) Into the woods to look for flowers and small animals.

         (b) To a zoo if one is near the school.

         (c) Star-gazing parties at the children's homes.

    C. List any changes of feelings toward any of the children or toward any of the teachers that you can attribute to this experience.

       (1) Some of the children who were shy and quiet in the classroom excelled at the outdoor school. Some of the more aggressive children, on the other hand, appeared more quiet away from the regular classroom situation.

       (2) My most outstanding changes were toward a certain boy and girl pupil. I was about to give up on the idea of getting along with them, when at the outdoor school they both seemed to accept me and they have been very cordial ever since.

2. List instances where you observed or participated in practical applications of principles of learning.

    A. I noticed that the children learned more by going out on hikes and actually getting specimens than by just reading about them. They seemed to get more from doing something they enjoyed doing. They were more eager to learn in the more relaxed atmosphere of the outdoor school than by just studying in the classroom.

    B. With the proper motivation the children see a need to use books and available material without being forced or told.

3. List instances when you have observed what you believe to be changes in a child's behavior which were attributable to the outdoor school experience.

    A. The children who were very quiet in the classroom, or seemed disinterested in school, suddenly came to life. It seemed that they couldn't get enough information about the subject they were interested in.

    B. If a child found a rock, no matter how many rocks of the same kind had been found, his rock was very special to him. He prized it as though it were gold and the only rock of its kind in the world.

4. What changes would you suggest if we were to plan an outdoor education program such as this again?

    A. Have a longer outdoor school period. Five days is good for the children, but it just skims the top of the subjects studied and does not allow sufficient time for depth.

    B. Try to obtain more reference books on plants written on the children's level.

5. List anything you have learned or any change on your part that has not been indicated by the above questions.

    A. I couldn't help thinking what a wonderful experience it was for all of us. We were living in a different environment which was completely new to most of us. Here we each had a purpose. Our purpose was to actually see and learn more about the things we have read about in books.

    B. The outdoor school experience is invaluable. The children seem to learn so much and they enjoy it, too. They get so interested in what they are doing that you begin to wonder if these are the same children you have in the classroom.

C. This was one of the most profitable experiences that I have ever had. It tied together what I have been learning in my college classes. The children found out that learning is fun and that you don't need a book in order to learn; you can learn from your environment. Even as small and seemingly insignificant as the ant is, we can still learn many things from him.

D. In the outdoor school environment the children saw their teachers in a completely different light. They saw that teachers were human and were just as interested in the subjects to be studied as they were. Both were learning together.

RESEARCH FINDINGS

The growth of outdoor education over the past four decades has been paralleled by a slowly growing body of information. According to a summary of doctoral dissertations prepared for the AAHPER Outdoor Education Project, most of the studies fall into five major groupings: (1) proposals for new program developments; (2) organization and administration; (3) historical analysis; (4) teacher education; and (5) evaluation. A few of these investigations contain findings that are of significance to the outdoor educator.

PROGRAM EVALUATION

● Sharp (1947) was involved in an experiment undertaken by the Board of Education of the City of New York in cooperation with Life Camps. A small-scale experimental design was developed using fifth and seventh grade pupils in a three-week resident outdoor education program. One of the major questions that were explored in this research project was, "Is educational camping an effective medium for meeting the objectives of education?"

A wide variety of tests and other measurement techniques were employed on a before-and-after basis that provided objective, semi-objective, and clinical data. The results revealed:

1. Gains from initial to final testing that were statistically significant, favored the experimental group in two areas: Interest Inventory (7th grade); vocabulary (5th grade.)

2. On the initial testing, prior to camp, the experimental group scored higher in each of the tests and Interest Inventory in both the fifth and seventh grades. Four of the differences were statistically significant: Interest Inventory (7th); science and health education, nature study, and Interest Inventory (5th).

3. On the final testing, after camp, the experimental group scored higher on eight of the ten comparisons. Five differences, all favoring the experimental group, were statistically significant: Interest Inventory (7th); nature study, vocabulary, arithmetic, and Interest Inventory (5th).

4. Language Arts: The experimental group displayed gains over the control group in written expression in interest value, style, vocabulary, and types of activities described.

5. Artistic Representation: Experimental group drawings indicated more enriched concepts, increased visual impressions, and some improvement in artistic ability.

6. "Guess Who." The results were essentially that the camping experience did not change the role of outstanding children, such as leaders or showoffs.

7. Counselor Records. The most striking result was that many insights about the children were attained by the staff within the very brief camping period.

Although there were several limitations to this study, the implications from the data were that the experimental groups benefited in some ways that were not possible in the regular "indoor" school program.

● Cragg (1952) attempted to determine the development of sixth grade campers as compared to non-campers and to appraise the educational achievements of the camp program in terms of the educational objectives identified by the school. Cragg's general conclusions were:

I. In spite of the shortness of the resident outdoor school period (one week), some definite contributions to the educational development of the children were made.

   A. Intellectual Development

      1. Nature Study: the camp group showed greater improvement than those who remained in the classroom.

   B. Physical Health

      1. The camp maintains an environment that is healthful for the majority of the children.

   C. Social Relationships

      1. Boys demonstrated more stability in their friendship patterns and seem to maintain more continuity in leadership than girls.

      2. Certain children maintain leadership roles and certain children remain social isolates regardless of their environment.

   D. Emotional Development

      1. The camping experience produced a strong emotional impact in the joy and enthusiasm aroused in the children.

II. The experience holds elements of uniqueness common to many of the children; but the reaction to the experience is varied, individualistic, and enthusiastic. Experiences at camp which hold significance for children tend to retain this significance over a period of time.

● Hollenbeck (1958) obtained the following results in a study related to the educational outcomes of the school camp:

I. Art: the jury which compared the drawings of the outdoors made by the children before and after the camp experience found that:
   a) There was no significant change in the number of items illustrated but the activities pictured in the post-camp drawings included more on science topics.
   b) Post-camp drawings depicted different species of trees, canyons, and forested mountains to a greater extent than the pre-camp drawings.
   c) Pre-camp drawings showed the use of adult techniques and symbols, and a diffused effort to depict the outdoors. Post-camp drawings were more detailed and realistic.
   d) Post-camp drawings disclosed a better understanding of the kinds of life found in the outdoors and keener powers of observation of the children.
II. Interest: An analysis of the pre-camp and post-camp scores on the interest inventory revealed that:
   a) Fifth grade children made significant gains in science interests.
   b) Fifth grade boys showed gains in all eight areas of the inventory: art, music, social studies, active play, quiet play, manual arts, home arts, and science.

SUBJECT MATTER AREAS/COGNITIVE DOMAIN

● Pike (1954) developed a science test that could be used to evaluate the science program in an outdoor school. The test was given to 207 sixth grade pupils two weeks before camp and again the week after they returned to school. The most significant gains were made in the general areas of knowledge of plant relationships and rocks and minerals. The poorest showings were made in the areas of conservation concepts and general camping knowledge and skills.

● Evans (1957) investigated the effects of a six-week summer camp arithmetic enrichment experience on the achievement of thirty elementary school boys. The Stanford Achievement Test in Arithmetic was used for both pre- and post-testing the experimental and control groups that had been matched according to age, achievement scores in arithmetic, and I.Q. The findings indicated:

   a) A statistically significant difference toward the experimental group in all categories.

b) The experimental group showed a significantly smaller loss of arithmetic ability over the summer period as compared to the control group.

SOCIALIZATION/AFFECTIVE DOMAIN

● Cole (1957) designed a study that had a twofold purpose: (1) to determine whether a work-learn camp for potential high school dropouts had greater holding power than the regular school program for a comparable group of potential school leavers who remained in school; and (2) to find out to what extent students might improve in their home, school, and social adjustments following the camp experience. The experiment involved three sample groups: (a) potential dropouts who participated in the work-learn camp experience; (b) potential dropouts who remained in school; and (c) a well-adjusted group that also remained in school. The first group spent more than half the year in the work-learn camp.

The major finding was improved attitudes toward school. At the beginning of the camp experience, the majority of the camper group was openly hostile to school and everyone connected with it. After camp, over half the group indicated they planned or had the desire to complete their education. Forty per cent said that they appreciated school more after the experience at camp. Classes were easier for 21 per cent of the camper group and the relationships between students and teachers had improved 46 per cent. Peer relationships improved for 36 per cent of the campers after their return from camp. Ninety-three per cent of the campers indicated that they would repeat the experience.

Although fewer campers remained to graduate than the other two groups (camp group = 32%; comparison group in school = 60%; well-adjusted group in school = 97%) those who did apparently felt that the camp experience was responsible for their remaining in school to complete their education.

● Kranzer (1958) created an experimental design that would measure the effects (social, emotional, intellectual, physical, democratic group living) of a one-week resident outdoor school program for sixth graders.

He concluded after obtaining data with Woods's "Behavior Preference Record," the "Haggerty-Olson-Wichman Behavior Rating Scale," and sociograms that social and democratic behavioral changes take place more rapidly during a week of school camping than during a regular "indoor" school program. A slight improvement in critical thinking was made by low mental ability students. There was also an increase in the number of isolates in camp beyond what would normally be found in the classroom.

● Beker (1959) evaluated the effects of a school camping experience upon pupils' self-concepts and social relationships. He used the "Classroom Social

Distance Scale" and a "Fifty-six Item Self-Concept Check List" as instruments on a before-and-after basis.

The findings indicated that the experimental group gained more positive feelings toward themselves after the outdoor school experience. These changes were also greater than those of the control group. Positive gains were also indicated in the area of social relationships of the experimental group. These social relationship patterns increased even more when measured again ten weeks later.

• Stack (1964) tested fifth and sixth grade students from a lower-middle socio-economic background before-and-after a one week resident outdoor school experience in order to assess attitudes toward selected concepts of school, teachers, self, classmates, friends, and school camping. Some of his findings were:

1. There was a consistent change of attitude of both grades in a positive manner toward the homeroom teacher, subsequent to camp.
2. Boys changed more favorably in regard to the homeroom teacher than did girls, after camp.
3. There was an overall change in students in a more positive attitude toward school camping, subsequent to the experience.
4. Students considered getting better acquainted as one of the most important features of the experience.
5. There was an overall positive gain in relation to attitudes towards friends . . . with boys forming more friendships following camp than did girls.

The following conclusions were justified by Stack's study:

1. Despite its limited duration, greater freedom of choice of companions and an increase in the number of friendships formed characterized the school camp program.
2. The school camp experience provided unique opportunities for affecting social change, particularly where the problem of racial cleavage was a factor.
3. Although classmates of lowest sociometric rating received more recognition from classmates following camping, no appreciable improvement in the sociometric work companion ratings of neglectees and isolates was effected.
4. Both boys and girls regarded school more positively after camp, with widened friendship patterns exerting an influence for an improved emotional tone in the classroom.
5. The rapport between teachers and students was strengthened.
6. The educational camp, by its structure, increased the values of relationships and associations over those of "ego-concept."

7. For boys, particularly, school camping served as a new stimulus to rekindle interests in the important relationships regarding school, teachers, camping, self, and friends.

● Davidson (1965) measured changes in the social relationships and self-concepts of sixty, fifth and sixth grade children who participated in two philosophically different camp programs. Thirty children were randomly assigned to encampment I (Adult-Centered) which featured fixed schedules, inflexible programming, constrictive adult guidance, and a minimum of group interaction. The remaining thirty took part in encampment II (Child-Centered) which encouraged individual initiative, group interaction, self-government, flexible programming, and a minimum of adult interference.

Changes in Self-Concept: The more highly-structured and constrictive encampment I showed more positive group shifts than did the less structured encampment II. Both encampments produced positive gains measured by a self-concept check list. What may be concluded from these data is not that one camp was better or worse than the other camp, but that one camp produced certain changes in self-concepts that were not produced in the other camp.

Social Relationships: Encampment II had a higher proportion of changes in peer relationships than did encampment I. The data seem to indicate that school camping has a positive influence on the acceptance of classmates regardless of the emphasis of the curriculum or the philosophical orientation of the camp. Slight differences favoring the less-structured encampment (Child-Centered) were not found to be statistically significant over the more highly-structured, adult-centered camp. However, it seems that II exerted a more positive influence on children's peer relationships than did the adult-centered camp.

The school camp with its emphasis on cooperative endeavors and close harmony in work situations apparently produces an environment for decreasing the social distance between high and low status children. Observations indicated that low status children were eagerly sought out at camp because of their willingness to work cooperatively in community group projects. Of course, it is possible to assume that these children were exploited by higher status children, but even if the basic motive was exploitation, it turned to genuine regard for these low status children who were so willing and eager to help.

ORGANIZATION AND ADMINISTRATION

● Sharp (1930) experimented with the summer camp as a setting for achieving educational goals. After four years of operating Life Camps, he included the following recommendations in his conclusions:

1. Children should stay at the camps for more than two weeks.
2. The camping season should be lengthened, and the camps should be opened during weekends and holidays.

3. Additional camps should be opened to accommodate minority children and the various age groups of both children and adults.

● Christman (1957) using the historical and normative survey method of investigation concluded:

1. Camping programs should serve all age levels.
2. Pupils should attend camp of their own volition.
3. The school camp should be coeducational.
4. The school camp should not exceed forty pupils.

● Schafer (1965) developed guidelines for the initiation and operation of outdoor education programs. Using a survey-questionnaire instrument, he gathered data from 172 resident outdoor schools. His major findings indicated:

1. Initiatory planning must be supported by administrators and teachers and be broadly based.
2. Programs should be seen as integral parts of the total school operation.
3. Leaders should have teaching skill, content knowledge, and previous experience in such programs.
4. School districts should consider the joint operation of regional outdoor schools, or leasing facilities in order to provide better programs and to reduce costs.
5. Objective evaluation techniques consistent with maintaining a flexible program should be used.

TEACHER EDUCATION

● Hauserman (1963) compared the classroom performances of student teachers who had an orientation to outdoor education with those who did not have this orientation. He found that: (1) the student teacher group with an outdoor orientation revealed a statistically greater behavioral pattern in the teaching-learning processes used; (2) the OSCAR, an observational instrument, showed a statistical difference in the emotional climate in the two groups. Student teachers with an outdoor orientation had consistently warmer, personal climates with greater emphasis on individual activities.

● Heppel (1964) investigated the changes in college juniors after they had experienced five days at a resident outdoor school with children by utilizing a questionnaire, daily logs, and an attitude scale of teaching values. Listed among her findings were:

1. Students who were majoring in elementary education generally reacted differently from secondary majors.

2. All students experienced anxiety the first two days, but this gave way to confidence later in the week.
3. Attitudes expressed as changed included awareness to a different environment, appreciation for informal group activities, individual differences, insights into children's interest spans, cooperativeness, eagerness, and personality fluctuations.
4. Elementary education majors generally formed more positive attitudes toward a camping program than did the secondary majors.

● Chase (1967) designed a study (1) to identify changes in the attitudes of school administrators (Williamson County, Illinois) toward the usefulness of outdoor education in achieving academic goals, and (2) to identify the changes in attitudes of the elementary teachers toward the usefulness of outdoor education in achievement of academic goals by their students.

The population tested was comprised of classroom teachers (165 public and private school teachers, K-6) and administrators employed during the 1967-68 academic year. The pre-test results were utilized in designing a program that would encourage teachers to use outdoor education techniques when appropriate. The basis for determining any significant changes in attitudes toward outdoor education was an instrument based upon the book, *Teaching in the Outdoors,* by Hammerman and Hammerman (1964). The philosophy developed in this book was assumed by the researcher to be the philosophy of outdoor education.

The following conclusions were drawn from the findings of the study:

1. Following exposure to an outdoor education program, there was less disparity between staffs of the districts in their attitude toward outdoor education.
2. All school staffs tested showed a significant increased belief in the Hammermans' attitude toward outdoor education.
3. The classroom teachers examined evidenced an acceptance of the Hammermans' philosophy that outdoor education in the schools is an integral part of the curriculum and involves an extension of the classroom to an outdoor laboratory.
4. The population of educators tested showed significant positive changes in attitude toward the use of outdoor education as a teaching aid in arithmetic, social studies, natural sciences, earth sciences, health-physical education-recreation, and the arts-crafts-music.

The study also concluded that if teacher training institutions would provide future teachers with outdoor education experiences, they would be well received.

SUMMARY

Since its inception, many claims have repeatedly been made for outdoor education. Unfortunately, not all these claims have been properly substantiated through valid research and evaluation procedures. Educators must continually submit their propositions and hypotheses concerning outdoor education to the rigors of empirical research. Only after such critical evaluations can effective programs be developed that will be relevant for various groups of children. Although the total number of evaluation and experimental studies is not large at the present time, more and more are gradually being designed and implemented.

SELECTED READINGS

*Ashcroft, Holly J. "The Attitude of Children Toward Outdoor Education." *California Journal of Elementary Education* 26:96-101, November, 1957.

Beker, Jerome. "The Relationship Between School Camping, Social Climate and Change in Children's Self-Concepts and Patterns of Social Relationship." Unpublished doctoral dissertation, Teachers College, Columbia University, 1959.

Chase, Craig C. "Changes in Attitude Toward Outdoor Education by Teachers and Administrators After Participation in the Cooperative Outdoor Education Project." Unpublished doctoral dissertation, Southern Illinois University, 1967.

Christman, John H. "The Administration of a Public Elementary School Camping and Outdoor Education Program." Unpublished doctoral dissertation, University of Buffalo, 1957.

Cole, Roy. "An Evaluation Study of an Extramural School Camping Program for Adolescent Boys Identified as Potential School Leavers." Unpublished doctoral dissertation, Wayne State University, 1957.

Cragg, Nadine A. "An Evaluation of the Year Round School Camp of Long Beach." Unpublished doctoral dissertation, University of Michigan, 1953.

*Davis, O.L. "The Effect of a School Camp Experience on Friendship Choices." *The Journal of Educational Sociology* 33:305-13, March, 1960.

Evans, Forrest F. "The Effects of a Summer Camp Arithmetic Enrichment Program." Unpublished doctoral dissertation, George Peabody College for Teachers, 1957.

Goodrich, Lois. "As Campers See It." *Bulletin of the National Association of Secondary School Principals* 31:21-30, May, 1947.

*Hammerman, Donald R. "Research Implications for Outdoor Education." *Journal of Health, Physical Education, Recreation* 35:89-90, March, 1964.

*These articles may be found in *Outdoor Education: A Book of Readings* by Hammerman and Hammerman (Minneapolis: Burgess Publishing Company, 1973).

Hammerman, Donald R., et al. "Research in Outdoor Education." AAHPER Outdoor Education Project, Washington, D.C., 1969.

Hauserman, Billy D. "The Effect of an Orientation to the Outdoor on Teaching Behavior in the Classroom." Unpublished doctoral dissertation, State University of New York, Buffalo, 1963.

Hendee, John C. "Challenging the Folklore of Environmental Education." *Journal of Environmental Education:* 3(3):19-23, Spring, 1972.

Heppel, Ruth. "Determining Changes College Students Undergo in Selected Categories as a Result of the School Camping Experience." Unpublished doctoral dissertation, Wayne State University, 1964.

*Hoeksema, Harold L. "Arithmetic Outdoors—It Does Make a Difference!" *Illinois Journal of Education* 55:18-19, December, 1964.

Hollenbeck, Irene E. "A Report of an Oregon School Camp with Program Emphasis Upon Outdoor Science Experiences." Unpublished doctoral dissertation, University of Colorado, 1958.

*Howenstine, William L. "Conservation in School Camping." *American Biology Teacher,* 24:40-5, January, 1962.

Kranzer, Herman C. "Effects of School Camping on Selected Aspects of Pupil Behavior—An Experimental Study." Unpublished doctoral dissertation, University of California at Los Angeles, 1958.

*Laug, M., and T. E. Echert. "Do It Yourself Conservation and the Effect Upon Attitudes of Prospective Teachers." *American Biology Teacher* 24:50-55, January, 1962.

Mager, Robert F. *Preparing Instructional Objectives.* Palo Alto, California: Fearon Publishers, 1962.

New York City Board of Education. *Extending Education Through Camping.* New York: Life Camps, 1948.

Pike, Kenneth V. "The Development of a Science Teaching Program for the Long Beach School Camp Hi-Hill." Unpublished master's project, Long Beach State College, California, 1954.

Schafer, Frank G. "An Administrative Guide for Initiating Resident Outdoor Education in the Public Schools." Unpublished doctoral dissertation, Teachers College, Columbia University, 1965.

Sharp, Lloyd B. "Education and the Summer Camp—An Experiment." Unpublished doctoral dissertation, Teachers College, Columbia University, 1930.

*These articles may be found in *Outdoor Education:* a book of readings by Hammerman and Hammerman (Minneapolis: Burgess Publishing Company, 1973).